Obama and the Empire

Obama and the Empire

Fidel Castro

New, expanded edition

Ocean Press
Melbourne ▪ New York ▪ London
www.oceanbooks.com.au

Cover design: Runa Kamijo

ISBN 978-0-9870779-1-2
Library of Congress Catalog Card Number: 2011940648

First edition published in 2010
Expanded, second edition published in 2012

Published in Spanish as *Obama y el imperio* 978-1-921700-00-2

Printed in the United States

PUBLISHED BY OCEAN PRESS

PO Box 1015, North Melbourne, VIC 3051, Australia
E-mail: info@oceanbooks.com.au

OCEAN PRESS TRADE DISTRIBUTORS

United States: **Consortium Book Sales and Distribution**
Tel: 1-800-283 3572 www.cbsd.com

Canada: **Publishers Group Canada**
Tel: 1-800-663 5714 E-mail: customerservice@raincoast.com

Australia and New Zealand: **Palgrave Macmillan**
Tel: 1-300-135 113 E-mail: customer.service@macmillan.com.au

UK and Europe: **Turnaround Publisher Services**
Tel: (44) 020-8829 3000 E-mail: orders@turnaround-uk.com

Cuba and Latin America: **Ocean Sur**
E-mail: info@oceansur.com

CONTENTS

Publisher's Note

The main lines of US politics never change abruptly, not even when control of the presidency and the two chambers of Congress moves from one party to the other. This fact has been proven historically. But there has never been an opportunity to see how another type of politician—one who doesn't fit the traditional male, white, Anglo-Saxon and generally Protestant model—would adapt himself or herself to fill that role. This opportunity has arisen with the election to the US presidency of Barack Obama.

Due to the racial and gender discrimination that exists in US society, the possibility of an African American or a woman being elected to the presidency could only be imagined after the extraordinary decade of social struggles of the 1960s: a decade of struggles for civil rights of African Americans, for women's liberation, for the social acceptance of the counterculture, against the Vietnam War and many other social movements. That is why there has been a tendency to consider the election of an African American or a woman as president as something progressive in itself. This notion was reinforced by symbolic presidential campaigns, such as those of Rev. Jesse Jackson in 1984 and 1988, that were initiated largely for mass education and mobilization purposes.

The deepening of the economic, social and moral crisis of the United States turned the miracle into reality. So much damage to the credibility of the political system was inherited from the presidencies of Ronald Reagan (1981-1989) to George W. Bush (2001-2009) that, since it was impossible to change the politics of the system, it became necessary to change the type—or stereotype—of the person in charge of carrying out that policy. Therefore, for the first time in history, in the 2008 presidential campaign, the real possibility emerged of an African American (Barack Obama) or a white woman (Hillary Clinton) being elected to the highest office in the United States. So it was that Obama was elected as the Democratic presidential candidate and then as president, but it could have been Hillary Clinton.

As it turned out, the miracle became reality, but not how the sixties generation dreamed it would be.

How should Obama's election to the presidency be understood and his performance during his first year and a half in office evaluated?

One of the world's political figures best qualified to answer these questions is Fidel Castro, the historic leader of the Cuban revolution that has successfully resisted the policy of aggression, blockade and isolation carried out against it by the United States for over 51 years.

Fidel Castro and the Cuban revolution have outlasted 10 US presidents since 1959. Barack Obama is now the 11th US president to confront the ongoing reality of Cuban revolution and has the opportunity to initiate a new relationship between island and the empire.

The editors
Ocean Press
2010

The Cynicism of the Empire

It would be dishonest of me to remain silent after hearing the speech Obama delivered on the afternoon of May 23 at the Cuban American National Foundation created by Ronald Reagan. I listened to his speech, as I did to McCain and Bush. I feel no resentment toward him, for he is not responsible for the crimes perpetrated against Cuba and humanity. If I were to defend him, I would do his adversaries an enormous favor. I therefore have no reservations about criticizing him and about expressing my point of view on his words frankly.

What did Obama say?

> "Throughout my entire life, there has been injustice in Cuba. Never, in my lifetime, have the people of Cuba known freedom. Never, in the lives of two generations of Cubans, have the people of Cuba known democracy. This is the terrible and tragic status quo that we have known for half a century—of elections that are anything but free or fair.... I won't stand for this injustice, you won't stand for this injustice, and together we will stand up for freedom in Cuba," he told the annexationists, adding: "It's time to let Cuban American money make their families less dependent upon the Castro regime.... I will maintain the embargo."

These statements by this strong candidate for the US presidency spare me the effort of having to explain the reason for this "Reflection."

José [Pepe] Hernández, one of the Cuban American National Foundation directors whom Obama praises in his speech, was none other than the owner of the 50-calibre automatic rifle, equipped with telescopic and infrared sights, which was confiscated, by chance, along with other deadly weapons while being transported by sea to Venezuela, where the foundation had planned to assassinate the writer of these lines at an international meeting held in Margarita, in the Venezuelan state of Nueva Esparta.

Pepe Hernández's group wanted to renegotiate a former pact with [President] Clinton, betrayed by [Jorge] Mas Canosa's clan, who secured Bush's electoral victory in 2000 through fraud, because the latter had promised to assassinate Castro, something they all happily embraced. This is the kind of political chicanery inherent in the decadent and contradictory US political system.

Presidential candidate Obama's speech may be summarized as follows: hunger for the [Cuban] nation, remittances as charitable hand-outs and visits to Cuba as propaganda for the consumerist and unsustainable US way of life.

How does he plan to address the extremely serious problem of the food crisis? The world's grains must be distributed among human beings, domestic animals and fish; our fish stocks are becoming smaller every year and more scarce in seas that have been overexploited by the large trawlers that no international organization can obstruct. Producing meat from gas and oil is no easy feat. Even Obama overestimates technology's potential in the fight against climate change, though he is more conscious of the risks and the limited time frame than Bush. He could seek the advice of [Al] Gore, who is also a Democrat and no longer a candidate, as he is aware of the accelerated pace at which global warming is advancing. His close political rival Bill Clinton, who is not running for the presidency, an expert on extra-territorial laws like the Helms-Burton and Torricelli Acts, can advise him on an issue like the blockade [against Cuba] that he promised to lift and never did.

What did he say in his speech in Miami, this man who, undoubtedly, from a social and human point of view, is the most progressive US presidential candidate? "For 200 years," he said, "the United States has made it clear that we won't stand for foreign intervention in our hemisphere. But every day, across the Americas, there is a different kind of struggle—not against foreign armies, but against the deadly threat of hunger and thirst, disease and despair. That is not a future that we have to accept—not for the child in Port au Prince or the family in the highlands of Peru. We can do better. We must do better.... We cannot ignore suffering to our south, nor stand for the globalization of the empty stomach." A magnificent description of imperialist globalization: "The globalization of the empty stomach!" We should thank him for this. But, 200 years ago, Bolívar fought for Latin American unity and, more than 100 years ago, Martí gave his life in the struggle against the annexation of Cuba by the United States. What is the difference between what Monroe proclaimed and what Obama has revived in his speech proclaimed two centuries later?

"I will reinstate a Special Envoy for the Americas in my White House who will work with my full support. But we will also expand the Foreign Service, and open more consulates in the neglected regions of the Americas. We will expand the Peace Corps, and ask more young Americans to go abroad to deepen the trust and the ties among our people," he said toward the end of his remarks, concluding: "Together, we can choose the future over the past." A beautiful phrase, for it attests to the idea, or at least the fear, that history makes personalities what they are and not all the way around.

Today, the United States has nothing of the spirit behind the Philadelphia declaration of principles formulated by the 13 colonies that rebelled against English colonialism. Today, it is a gigantic empire that could never have been imagined by the country's original founders. Nothing, however, was to change for the indigenous people and the slaves. The former were exterminated as the nation expanded; the latter continued to be auctioned in the marketplaces—men, women and children—for nearly a century, despite the fact that "all men are born free and equal," as the Declaration of Independence affirms. The objective conditions of the world favored the development of that system.

In his speech, Obama portrays the Cuban revolution as anti-democratic and lacking in respect for freedom and human rights. It is the exact same argument which, almost without exception, US administrations have used time and again to justify their crimes against our country. The blockade, in and of itself, is an act of genocide. I don't want to see US children inculcated with those shameful values.

An armed revolution in our country might not have been needed without all the military interventions, the Platt Amendment and economic colonialism visited upon Cuba.

The revolution was the result of imperial domination. We cannot be accused of having imposed it upon Cuba. Real change could have and ought to have been brought about in the United States. Its own workers, more than a century ago, voiced the demand for an eight-hour workday that arose with the development of productive forces.

The first thing the leaders of the Cuban revolution learned from [José] Martí was to believe in and act on behalf of an organization founded for the purpose of bringing about a revolution. We were always bound by previous forms of power and, following the institutionalization of this organization, we were elected by more than 90 percent of voters, as has become customary in Cuba, a process that does not in the least resemble the ridiculous level of electoral participation which often—such as in the United States—remains less than 50 percent of the voters. No small and blockaded country like ours would have been able to hold its ground for so long on the basis of ambition, vanity, deceit or the abuse of power, the kind of power that exists in its neighbor. To state otherwise insults the intelligence of our heroic people.

I am not questioning Obama's great intelligence, his debating skills or his work ethic. He is a talented orator and is ahead of his rivals in the electoral race. I feel sympathy for his wife and little girls, who accompany him and give him encouragement every Tuesday. It is indeed a touching human spectacle. Nevertheless, I am obliged to raise a number of delicate questions. I do not expect answers; I only wish to raise them for the record.

1. Is it right for the president of the United States to order the assassination of any other person in the world, whatever the pretext may be?
2. Is it ethical for the president of the United States to order the torture of other human beings?
3. Should state terrorism be used by a country as powerful as the United States as an instrument to bring about peace on the planet?
4. Is an Adjustment Act, applied as punishment against only one country, Cuba, in order to destabilize it, good and honorable, even when it costs the lives of innocent children and mothers? If it is good, why is this right not automatically granted to Haitians, Dominicans, and other peoples of the Caribbean, and why isn't the same act applied to Mexicans and people from Central and South America, who die like flies against the Mexican border wall or in the waters of the Atlantic and the Pacific?
5. Can the United States do without immigrants, who grow vegetables, fruits, almonds and other delicacies for US citizens? Who would sweep their streets, work as servants in their homes or do the worst and lowest-paid jobs?
6. Are crackdowns on illegal residents fair, even as they affect children born in the United States?
7. Is the brain drain—the continuous theft of the best scientific and intellectual minds from poor countries—moral and justifiable?
8. You state, as I pointed out at the beginning of this "Reflection," that your country had long ago warned European powers that it would not tolerate any intervention in the hemisphere, reiterating that this right must be respected while demanding the right to intervene anywhere in the world with the aid of

hundreds of military bases and naval, air and space forces distributed across the planet. I ask: Is that the way in which the United States expresses its respect for freedom, democracy and human rights?

9. Is it fair to stage pre-emptive attacks on 60 or more dark corners of the world, as Bush calls them, whatever the pretext may be?
10. Is it honorable and sane to invest millions and millions of dollars in the military industrial complex to produce weapons that can destroy life on earth several times over?

Before judging our country, you should know that Cuba, with its education, health, sports, culture and sciences programs, implemented not only in its own territory but also in other poor countries around the world, and the blood that has been shed in acts of solidarity with other peoples, in spite of the economic and financial blockade and the aggression of your powerful country, is proof that much can be done with very little. Not even our closest ally, the Soviet Union, was able to achieve what we have.

The only form of cooperation the United States can offer other nations consists in sending military professionals to those countries. It cannot offer anything else, for it lacks a sufficient number of people willing to sacrifice themselves for others and offer substantial aid to a country in need (though Cuba has known and relied on the cooperation of excellent US doctors). They are not to blame for this, for society does not inculcate such values in them on a massive scale.

We have never subordinated cooperation with other countries to ideological requirements. We offered the United States our help when hurricane Katrina lashed the city of New Orleans. Our internationalist medical brigade bears the glorious name of Henry Reeve, a young man, born in the United States, who fought and died for Cuba's sovereignty in our first war of independence.

Our revolution can mobilize tens of thousands of doctors and health workers. It can mobilize an equally vast number of teachers and citizens, who are willing to travel to any corner of the world to fulfill any noble purpose, not to usurp people's rights or take possession of raw materials.

The goodwill and determination of the people constitute limitless resources that cannot be kept in, and would not fit into, the vault of a bank. They cannot spring from the hypocritical politics of an empire.

May 25, 2008

The November 4 Elections

Tomorrow will be a significant day. The world will be following the elections in the most powerful nation on earth, the United States. Right now, with less than 5 percent of the world's population the United States every year swallows huge amounts of oil and gas, minerals, raw materials, consumer goods and sophisticated products brought from overseas. Many of these, particularly fuel and minerals extracted from mines, are nonrenewable.

The United States is the largest arms producer and exporter. Its industrial military complex also has an insatiable domestic market. Its naval and air forces are deployed in scores of military basis located in the territory of other nations. The US strategic missiles carry warheads that can reach any place in the world with absolute precision.

A great number of the cleverest minds in the world are uprooted from their original countries and placed at the service of this system. It is a parasitical and plundering empire.

It is a known fact that the black population introduced into the United States throughout centuries of slavery is the victim of significant racial discrimination.

The Democratic candidate Obama is partly black; the dark skin and features of that race are obvious in him. He was able to study at a higher education institution where he graduated with outstanding marks. He is certainly more clever, better educated and sanguine than his Republican adversary.

Tomorrow's elections take place when the world is enduring a serious financial crisis—the worst since the 1930s—among many others that have seriously affected the economy of many nations in the course of three-quarters of a century.

The international media, political analysts and commentators are using part of their time to discuss the issue. Obama is considered to be the best US political orator for decades. His compatriot Toni Morrison, a 1993 Nobel Prize laureate in literature, and the first from her ethnic group born in the United States to be awarded such prize, has called him the future president and poet of that nation.

I have been watching the struggle between the contestants. The black candidate caused much amazement when he was nominated in the face of strong opposition. He has well-articulated ideas that he hammers again and again into voters' minds. He does not hesitate to claim that more than Republicans or Democrats they are all Americans, citizens he describes as the most productive in the world. He says he will reduce taxes for the middle class, in which he includes practically everybody, while he will completely eliminate taxes for the poorest sectors and raise them for the wealthiest. The revenues, he claims, will not the used to bail out banks.

He insists repeatedly that the ruinous spending on Bush's war in Iraq will not be paid by American taxpayers. He will put an end to that war and bring the US troops back home. Perhaps he is mindful of the fact that Iraq had nothing to do with the terrorist attacks of September 11, 2001. Nevertheless, the blood has been shed of thousands of US troops, injured or killed in battle, and the lives lost of over a million people in that Muslim nation. This was a war of conquest imposed by the empire in its search for oil.

In light of the current financial crisis and its consequences, the US people are more concerned about the economy than the war in Iraq. They are anxious about their jobs, the safety of their bank deposits and their retirement funds, and fearful of losing the purchasing power of their money and the houses where they live with their families. They want the certainty that whatever the circumstances they will receive adequate medical care and that their children will be able to access higher education.

Obama is presenting a challenge, and I think he has taken and will still take great risks in a country where any extremist can legally purchase a sophisticated modern weapon anywhere, as it was in the first half of the 18th century in the American West. He supports the system and he will get support from it. The pressing problems of the world are not really a major source of concern to Obama, much less to the other candidate who, as a war pilot, dropped tens of tons of bombs on Hanoi (more than 9,375 miles from Washington) for which he has no remorse.

When, last Thursday, in a letter to [President] Lula [da Silva of Brazil], in addition to what I had already mentioned in my "Reflection" of October 31, I wrote: "Racism and discrimination have been present in US society since its birth over two centuries ago. Latin Americans and blacks have always been discriminated against there. Its citizens have been brought up in a consumer society. Humanity is objectively threatened by its weapons of mass extermination."

"The US people are more concerned about the economy than the Iraq war. McCain is an old, bellicose and uneducated man; he is not very smart and he is in poor health," I continued.

Finally, I said: "If my estimates are wrong and racism prevailed; if the Republican candidate won the presidency, the threat of war would increase and the opportunities for the peoples of the world to progress would be reduced. Nevertheless, we need to fight and to build awareness about this, whoever wins this election."

When these views of mine are published tomorrow, nobody will have time to say that I wrote something that could be used by any candidate to advance his campaign. I had to be, and I have been, neutral in this electoral contest. This is not "interference in the internal affairs of the United States," as the State Department would put it, but being respectful of other countries' sovereignty.

November 3, 2008

Swimming Against the Current

Following Obama's speech, on May 23 this year, to the Cuban American National Foundation established by Ronald Reagan, I wrote a "Reflection" entitled "The Empire's Hypocritical Politics" on May 25.

In that "Reflection" I quoted Obama's exact words to the Miami annexationists: "[T]ogether we will stand up for freedom in Cuba.... It's time to let Cuban American money make their families less dependent upon the Castro regime. *I will maintain the embargo.*"

I then offered several arguments and examples of the generally unethical behavior of the presidents who preceded the one who would be elected on November 4. I then wrote I was "obliged to raise a number of delicate questions." These were:

1. Is it right for the president of the United States to order the assassination of any other person in the world, whatever the pretext may be?
2. Is it ethical for the president of the United States to order the torture of other human beings?
3. Should state terrorism be used by a country as powerful as the United States as an instrument to bring about peace on the planet?
4. Is an Adjustment Act, applied as punishment against only one country, Cuba, in order to destabilize it, good and honorable, even when it costs the lives of innocent children

and mothers? If it is good, why is this right not automatically granted to Haitians, Dominicans, and other peoples of the Caribbean, and why isn't the same Act applied to Mexicans and people from Central and South America, who die like flies against the Mexican border wall or in the waters of the Atlantic and the Pacific?

5. Can the United States do without immigrants, who grow vegetables, fruits, almonds and other delicacies for US citizens? Who would sweep their streets, work as servants in their homes or do the worst and lowest-paid jobs?
6. Are crackdowns on illegal residents fair, even as they affect children born in the United States?
7. Is the brain drain—the continuous theft of the best scientific and intellectual minds from poor countries—moral and justifiable?
8. You state, as I pointed out at the beginning of this "Reflection," that your country had long ago warned European powers that it would not tolerate any intervention in the hemisphere, reiterating that this right must be respected while demanding the right to intervene anywhere in the world with the aid of hundreds of military bases and naval, air and space forces distributed across the planet. I ask: Is that the way in which the United States expresses its respect for freedom, democracy and human rights?
9. Is it fair to stage pre-emptive attacks on 60 or more dark corners of the world, as Bush calls them, whatever the pretext may be?
10. Is it honorable and sane to invest millions and millions of dollars in the military industrial complex, to produce weapons that can destroy life on earth several times over?

I could have included several other issues. Despite these pointed questions, I was not unkind to the African American candidate. I perceived he had greater ability and command of the art of politics compared not only to his adversaries in the [Republican] party but also to those in his own [Democratic] party.

Last week, the US President-elect Barack Obama announced his economic recovery program.

On Monday December 1 he introduced his National Security and Foreign Policy teams, stating:

> "Today, Vice-President-elect Biden and I are pleased to announce our national security team.... Our old conflicts remain unresolved. And newly asserted powers have put strains on the international system.
>
> "The spread of nuclear weapons raises the peril that the world's deadliest technology could fall into dangerous hands. Our dependence on foreign oil empowers authoritarian governments and endangers our planet....
>
> "[O]ur economic power must sustain our military strength, our diplomatic leverage, and our global leadership....
>
> "We will renew old alliances and forge new and enduring partnerships.... American values are America's greatest export to the world....
>
> "The team that we have assembled here today is uniquely suited to do just that.... [T]hese men and women represent all of those elements of American power.... They have served in uniform and as diplomats.... They share my pragmatism about the use of power, and my sense of purpose about America's role as a leader in the world."

"I have known Hillary Clinton as a friend," he says. I am mindful of the fact that she was President-elect Barack Obama's rival and the wife of President Clinton, who signed the extraterritorial Torricelli and Helms Burton Acts against Cuba. During the presidential race she committed herself to these laws and to the economic blockade. I am not complaining, I am simply stating this for the record.

"I am proud that she will be our next secretary of state," said Obama. "[She] will command respect in every capital; and ... will clearly have the ability to advance our interests around the world. Hillary's appointment is a sign to friend and foe of the seriousness of my commitment..."

> "At a time when we face an unprecedented transition amidst two wars, I have asked Robert Gates to continue as secretary of defense....
>
> "I will be giving Secretary Gates and our military a new mission as soon as I take office: responsibly ending the war in Iraq through a successful transition to Iraqi control."

It strikes me that Gates is a Republican, not a Democrat. He is the only one who has been secretary of defense and director of the Central Intelligence Agency, that is, he has occupied these positions under both Democratic and Republican administrations. Gates, who is aware of his popularity, has said he first made sure that the president-elect was choosing him for as long as necessary.

On the other hand, while Condoleezza Rice was traveling to India and Pakistan under Bush's instructions to mediate in the tense relations between these two countries, two days ago, the minister of defense from Brazil gave the green light to a Brazilian company to manufacture MAR-1 missiles; but instead of one a month, as had been the case until now, it will produce five every month. One hundred of these missiles will be sold to Pakistan at an estimated cost of 85 million euros.

In a public statement, the minister said, "these missiles that can be attached to planes have been designed to locate ground radars. They allow the effective monitoring of both the ground and air space."

As for Obama, he continued on regardless with his statement on Monday: "And going forward, we will continue to make the investments necessary to strengthen our military and increase our ground forces to defeat the threats of the 21st century."

On Janet Napolitano, he said: "[She] offers the experience and executive skill that we need in the next secretary of homeland security.... Janet assumes this critical role having learned the lessons, some of them painful, of the last several years, from 9/11 to Katrina.... She understands as well as anyone the danger of an insecure border. And she will be a leader who can reform a sprawling department while safeguarding our homeland."

This familiar figure had been appointed a district attorney in Arizona by Clinton in 1993, and then promoted to state attorney general in 1998. Later, in 2002, she became a Democratic Party candidate and then governor of the border state that is the most common entry point for illegal immigrants. She was elected governor in 2006.

About Susan Elizabeth Rice, he said: "Susan knows that the global challenges we face demand global institutions that work... We need the United Nations to be more effective as a venue for collective action against terror and proliferation, climate change and genocide, poverty and disease."

On National Security Advisor James Jones he said: "I am convinced that General James Jones is uniquely suited to be a strong and skilled national security advisor. Generations of Joneses have served heroically on the battlefield from the beaches of Tarawa in World War II, to Fox Trot Ridge in Vietnam. Jim's Silver Star is a proud part of that legacy... He has commanded a platoon in battle, served as supreme allied commander in a time of war, [he means NATO and the Gulf War] and worked on behalf of peace in the Middle East."

> "Jim is focused on the threats of today and the future. He understands the connection between energy and national security, and has worked on the frontlines of global instability from Kosovo to northern Iraq to Afghanistan.
>
> "He will advise me and work effectively to integrate our efforts across the government, so that we are effectively using all elements of American power to defeat unconventional threats and promote our values.
>
> "I am confident that this is the team that we need to make a new beginning for American national security."

Obama is someone we can talk to—anywhere he wishes—since we do not preach violence or war. But he should be reminded that the stick and carrot doctrine will have no place in our country.

None of these phrases in his latest speech shows any element of a response to the questions I raised last May 25, just six months ago.

I will not say now that Obama is any less smart. On the contrary, he is showing the mental faculties that enabled me to see and compare his abilities with those of his mediocre adversary, John McCain, who was almost rewarded for his "exploits" merely due to the traditions of US society. If it had not been for the economic crisis, television and the Internet, Obama would not have won the elections against the omnipotence of racism. It also helped that Obama had studied first at Columbia University, where he graduated in political science, and then at Harvard where he graduated as a lawyer. This enabled him to become a member of the modestly wealthy class with only several million dollars. He is certainly not Abraham Lincoln, nor are these times similar to those. US society today is a consumer society where the saving habit has been lost while the spending habit has multiplied.

Somebody had to offer a calm and serene response even though this meant swimming against the current of the powerful stream of hope raised by Obama in international public opinion.

I only have two more press dispatches left to analyze. They include news from everywhere. I have estimated that in this economic crisis the United States alone will be spending over $6 trillion in paper money, an amount that can only be appreciated considering the sweat and hunger, suffering and blood of the rest of the world's peoples.

Our principles are the same as those of Baraguá. The empire should know that our homeland might be raised to the ground but the sovereign rights of the Cuban people are not negotiable.

December 4, 2008

The 11th President of the United States

This past Tuesday January 20, 2009, Barack Obama took on the leadership of the empire as the 11th president of the United States since the victory of the Cuban revolution in January 1959.

No one could doubt the sincerity of his words as he declared he would turn his country into a model of freedom and respect for human rights in the world and for the independence of other peoples. This, of course, could hardly offend anyone except for those misanthropes of the planet. He was relaxed in stating that the imprisonment and torture at the illegal Guantánamo base would cease immediately. This has raised doubts among those who rely on terror as an indispensable instrument of his country's foreign policy.

The intelligent and noble countenance of the first African-American president of the United States since its foundation as an independent republic, two and a third centuries ago, reflected his inspiration by the examples of Abraham Lincoln and Martin Luther King, Jr., to become the living symbol of the American dream.

Nevertheless, despite all he has been through, Obama has yet to face his main test: What will he do when the immense power he now has in his hands proves to be absolutely useless in order to overcome the insoluble antagonistic contradictions posed by the system?

January 22, 2009

Deciphering the Thoughts of the New US President

It is not too difficult. After taking office, Barack Obama said the decision to return to its legitimate owner of the territory occupied by the Guantánamo naval base required weighing up the extent to which the defensive capacity of the United States would or would not be affected.

Soon afterwards he added, with regard to the return to Cuba of the occupied territory, that he would first consider what concessions to demand from Cuba in return. This would amount to demanding a change of its political system, a price Cuba has been resisting for half a century.

To keep a military base in Cuba against the will of our people is a violation of the most elemental principles of international law. The US president has the ability to abide by that law without exacting any concession whatsoever. Non-compliance would be an act of arrogance and an abuse of his immense power against a small country.

For a better understanding of the abusive character of the power of the empire, consider the statements published on the US government's official website on January 22, 2009, after Barack Obama took up his post. [Vice-President] Biden and Obama have decided to resolutely support the relationship between the United States and Israel, and believe that the irrefutable commitment in the Middle East should be the security of Israel, the main US ally in the region.

The United States will never distance itself from Israel, and its president and vice-president "firmly believe in the right of Israel to protect its citizens," as was stated in the declaration of principles that reiterates this aspect of the policy followed by the government of George W. Bush, Obama's predecessor.

In this way, our friend Obama is complicit in the genocide against the Palestinians. Similar sweeteners have been offered to Russia, China, Europe, Latin America and the rest of the world, after the United States has turned Israel into a major nuclear power, a country that annually accounts for a significant share of the empire's booming military industry exports, with which they threaten, with extreme violence, the population of all Muslim countries.

Similar examples abound; there is no need to become a fortune teller. For further illustration, read the statements made by the new chief at the Pentagon, an expert in the business of war.

January 29, 2009

Contradictions Between Obama's Politics and Ethics

A few days ago I referred to some of Obama's ideas that point to his role in a system that denies every principle of justice.

Some throw their hands up in horror if any criticism is made of this important figure, even if it is done politely and with respect. This is usually accompanied by subtle and not so subtle darts from those with the means to throw and transform them into part of the media terror imposed on the peoples to sustain the unsustainable.

Every criticism I make is always construed as an attack, an accusation or something similar suggesting a callousness and discourtesy toward the person involved. This time I'd rather address some of the many questions that could be raised and that the new US president should answer. For example:

Whether or not he renounces his prerogative as president of the United States—a prerogative his predecessors with few exceptions exercised as a right *per se*—to order the assassination of a foreign political adversary, usually someone from an underdeveloped country?

By any chance, has any one of his many assistants ever informed him of the sinister actions [against Cuba] carried out by former presidents from Eisenhower onward, through the years 1960, 1961, 1962, 1963, 1964, 1965, 1966, and 1967 against Cuba, including the mercenary Bay of Pigs invasion, the terror campaigns, the introduction into our territory of a huge amount of weapons and ammunitions and other similar actions?

It is not my intention to blame the current president of the United States, Barack Obama, for actions conducted by former presidents when he had not even been born or when he was just a 6-year-old boy in Hawaii, a child born to a black Muslim Kenyan father and a white Christian American mother. On the contrary, this is an exceptional merit of US society and I am the first to admit it.

Is President Obama aware that for decades our country was the victim of deliberately introduced viruses and bacteria carrying diseases and plagues affecting people, animals and plants? Does he know that some of them, like the Hemorrhagic Dengue Fever, later became a scourge that took the lives of thousands of children in Latin America and that other plagues have an impact on the economy of the peoples of the Caribbean and the rest of the continent as collateral damage from which they have yet to recover?

Does he know that several politically submissive Latin American countries, which are today embarrassed by the damage they caused, also took part in such terrorist and economically harmful actions?

Why is our country the only one in the world enduring the imposition of a Cuban Adjustment Act which promotes trafficking in human beings and other actions that cost people's lives, mostly those of women and children?

Was it fair to impose on our people an economic blockade lasting almost 50 years?

Was it right to arbitrarily demand that the world accept the extraterritorial application of this economic blockade which can only bring hunger and shortages to the people?

The United States cannot meet its vital needs without extracting large mineral resources from a great many countries whose exports are restricted by the intermediate process of refining. In general, when it suits the interests of the empire, these products are traded by big transnational companies operating with Yankee capital.

Will that country renounce such privileges?

Would renunciation be compatible with the developed capitalist system?

When Mr. Obama promises to make large investments to be self-reliant in oil, despite the fact that his country today is the largest market in the world, what will the future be for those countries whose main revenues come from exporting energy resources as many of them lack any other significant source of income?

After the crisis, once the competition and the fight over markets and sources of employment is unleashed again, as is usually the case among those who are better off and monopolize technology with sophisticated means of production, what possibilities will be left to the undeveloped countries that dream of industrialization?

The efficiency of the new vehicles manufactured by the auto industry notwithstanding, will they use the technology demanded by the ecology to protect humanity from the increasing deterioration of the climate?

Will the blind philosophy of the market replace that which only rationality could promote?

Obama promises to mint enormous amounts of money to foster the quest for technologies that can multiply the production of energy without which modern societies would be paralyzed.

Nuclear power plants are among the sources of energy he promises to hastily develop. These are already opposed by a great many people due to the high risk of accidents with disastrous consequences for life, the environment and human food. Moreover, it is absolutely impossible to prevent some of these accidents occurring.

Modern industry has already contaminated all the seas on the planet with toxins, even without such disastrous accidents.

Can such contradictory and antagonistic interests be reconciled without transgressing ethics?

The US House of Representatives with a Democratic majority launched the extremely protectionist slogan of "buy US goods," to please the unions that supported his campaign. This tramples on a basic principle of the World Trade Organization, since every nation in the world, be they big or small, dreams of development through the trade of goods and services; however, only the big and rich among them have the privilege to be able to realize such a dream.

The Republicans in the United States, discredited by the actions of the reckless Bush administration, soon reacted against the measures taken by Obama to appease his allies in the unions. Thus the credibility of the new president of the United States is diminished in the eyes of voters.

As an old politician and combatant, I commit no sin by humbly exposing these ideas.

As hundreds of news items from the political, scientific and technological circles are published every day, many questions could be raised for which there are not easy answers.

February 4, 2009

A Quick Response

The response came hardly a few hours later in the voice of the White House Chief of Staff Rahm Emanuel. It doesn't matter that he chose not to mention my modest "Reflection." It is the response that counts.

He told journalists that it is the Cuban American community President Obama is interested in. This was the first time the subject had been addressed since the inauguration. Cubans with the right to vote, due to their heritage in the state of Florida, three to one voted for the Democratic candidate. Obama is not interested in the almost 12 million Cubans who live on the island.

When the man closest to the president was asked who he supported in Cuba he declined to elaborate, saying the less said on Cuba, the better.

He announced Cuban Americans will be permitted to travel to Cuba and to send remittances.

But he did not even mention US citizens' right to travel [to Cuba].

The Cuban Adjustment Act and the blockade deserved no comments from him.

Thus, sooner rather than later, Obama is losing his political virginity.

February 5, 2009

The G-20 Summit Opens

Today the G-20 Summit began. The experts in economic matters have made an enormous effort. Some, with experience in important international posts, others as learned researchers. The subject is a complex one, the language is new and demands that we familiarize ourselves with the terms, the economic facts, the international agencies and the political leaders who have the greatest weight on the international scene. Therefore, it is our desire to simplify and to explain intelligibly what is happening in London, as I see it.

Nobody was surprised that Obama was the star of the London summit. He represents the most powerful and wealthiest country in the world. He is favored by special circumstances. Bush – lying, cynical, war-mongering and vicious – is not there. Neither is McCain – mediocre and ignorant – thanks precisely to Obama's amazing [electoral] victory, a black man in the country of racial discrimination, where a majority of white voters cast their ballots for McCain, but not in enough numbers to compensate for the votes of more than 90 percent of black and mixed race Americans, citizens of Latino origin, the poor and those affected by the crisis. He has just been elected when other G-20 leaders are at the point of concluding their terms, and Obama will probably be the US president for the next eight years. Therefore, it is not strange that the news from London focuses on him.

What the world deems important is what comes out of the summit, that is, if anything comes out at all. Each of the participants has their own national and even personal objectives, as political leaders who will be judged by history.

Obama's objective is, in the first place, to change the image of his country, the party principally responsible for the tragedy the world is suffering and the party being rightly blamed for the current devastating economic crisis, in which he has absolutely no political responsibility. As Joseph Stiglitz, the former economic head of the International Monetary Fund and now MIT professor, points out: "He ought to come to say that he is guilty of nothing and that he is trying to solve it as quickly as he can."

His main European ally, British Prime Minister Gordon Brown, is the summit host, who is wildly hoping to alter the current anti-Labor tendency unleashed by the nonsense of his predecessor Tony Blair. Buckingham Palace honored Obama and his wife Michelle with a reception. The president gave the elderly queen a modern digital recorder, an example of sophisticated US technology (an iPod) with songs and images of the queen's state visit to the United States in 2007 and a book with musical scores signed by Richard Rogers. No words were exchanged with Her Highness about the mundane G-20 meeting.

Brown, on the other hand, is pulling out all stops with the crisis. He hopes to change the regulation of the banking system, promote economic growth, increase cooperation and end protectionism. He recognizes that the negotiations will be difficult.

His motto is: "Better to look forward than to look back." Clearly if the voters were to look back, he would win very few votes.

The desire of both allies at the heart of the G-20 Summit is to minimize the differences between France and Germany.

[French President] Sarkozy doesn't hide his displeasure with US policy. He is explosive. He recently threatened to walk out of the summit. Yesterday, on Europe Radio One, he declared that for now there is no satisfactory agreement at the summit, but he did soften his threats to leave the table if there is no move toward greater regulation, saying he would not "be associated with a summit that doesn't end with greater regulation." He confirmed that the negotiators have not reached any agreement.

The draft of the summit's communiqué, already circulating among journalists, refers to measures to reestablish global growth, keep markets open and encourage global trade. "We must get results, there is no choice," Sarkozy insisted yesterday.

A few days ago Obama announced that the United States proposes to introduce changes in its system of regulation and supervision, in the hope that this declaration would partly fulfill European demands, removing one of those issues.

Sarkozy responded stating he is serious about ending tax havens.

Very close to Sarkozy's position, Angela Merkel, the German chancellor, demands that the agreement includes neither the requirement of a tax stimulus plan for the advanced countries nor the instigation of a debate on the announcement of a new international currency which the emerging countries' are demanding of the G-7.

"The world is at a crossroads," Merkel said. "We must do everything possible so that the crisis is not repeated." "We have to go further than what was discussed in Washington," she added, saying everything agreed to in London must come with a guarantee that it will be applied. "There must not be one single place, or one single product or one single institution without supervision and transparency."

Merkel showed her commitment to increasing IMF funding and stepping up aid to developing countries which are largely suffering from the impact of the crisis.

Increasing IMF resources already appears to be a reality. When he arrived in London the Mexican president said he is negotiating a line of credit with the IMF for 26 billion euros. Yesterday in London John Lipsky, the number-two man in the International Monetary Fund, stated the fund would provide Mexico with a line of credit for $47 billion in order to guarantee the cash flow in case the market situation worsens because of the crisis. This figure is larger than that requested by Mexico.

As the United States has the majority of shares in the IMF, without its support such a line of credit would not be forthcoming and so this underpins Obama's influence at the London summit.

The news reports announced Obama would be meeting with Dmitri Medvedev and Hu Jintao, the presidents of Russia and China, to talk about the problems both countries have with the United States.

In the superpower's bilateral encounters with these two great powers, economic problems will certainly be tackled, and perhaps agreements that have been patiently discussed and approved through their diplomatic representatives will be announced.

Today, April 2, I read a long and detailed dispatch from the Xinhua News Agency from yesterday, reporting that "President Hu Jintao of China and President Barack Obama of the United States agreed today that their respective countries will work together to build a positive, cooperative and full relationship in the 21st century."

> "Furthermore, the presidents decided to establish the bilateral mechanism of Strategic and Economic Dialogues.
>
> "The new commitment, assumed by both heads of state during their meeting in London, will outline the direction and provide a major boost to sustained, solid and stable development of relations between the two nations.
>
> "The relationship between China and the United States continues to be one of the most important bilateral relationships in the world in the 21st century, one in which humankind faces enormous opportunities and challenges. In the new era, the two nations have important responsibilities in regards to world peace, stability and development and they also share wide interests.
>
> "The two parties ought to maintain the rhythm of the times and always conduct bilateral ties from a strategic, long-range perspective.
>
> "They must respect and take into consideration the fundamental interests of the other party and take advantage of opportunities, just as they must work together to face up to the challenges of the century.

> "Establishing the China-USA Strategic and Economic Dialogues mechanism is an important step to promote the bilateral relationship to an even greater extent. Thus, the earlier strategic dialogue between the two countries has been raised to a new level.
>
> "At a time when the international financial crisis continues to spread, the two nations must support one another and work together to weather the storm, and this will favor the primary mutual interests of China and the United States.
>
> "China and the United States should not only improve the exchanges and cooperation in areas such as the economy, the fight against terrorism, proliferation, transnational crime, climate change, energy and the environment, but they must also strengthen communication and coordination in regional and world issues."

Such an agreement cannot be discussed in a 60-minute meeting. All the details had already been drawn up.

China, whose allies today on the Asian continent invaded and plundered it only seven decades ago, is now moving to a top position in the world economy.

As the US's prime creditor, China calmly discusses with Obama the rules that will govern relations between two nations in a world fraught with risks.

Perhaps this Xinhua dispatch is one of the most important news items coming from the G-20 Summit.

April 2, 2009

Obama's Song

At a 2:30 press conference, Cuban time, after the G-20 Summit concluded, the US president declared that unemployment has reached its highest level in 26 years in his country. "Faced with similar global challenges in the past, the world was slow to act," he said.

> "Today we've learned the lessons of history… [S]ome of you in the press… confused honest and open debate with irreconcilable differences…. But… we have agreed on a series of unprecedented steps to restore growth and prevent a crisis like this from happening again…..
>
> "Number one, we are committed to growth and job creation…. The United States… [will] clean out the troubled assets… to ensure that our action leads directly to loans to businesses large and small. And… our G-20 partners are pursuing similarly comprehensive programs.
>
> "We also agreed on bold action to support developing countries [by giving them access to loans]….
>
> "We've also rejected the protectionism that could deepen the crisis.
>
> "We're extending supervision to all systemically important institutions…. And we will reform and expand the IMF and World Bank so they are more efficient, effective and representative."

Obama also said he intended to "work with Congress to provide $448 million in immediate assistance to vulnerable populations—from Africa to Latin America... [and] support the United Nations and World Bank as they coordinate the rapid assistance necessary to prevent humanitarian catastrophe."

The US president answered many direct questions from the accredited press as follows:

"Well, I think we did okay. You know, when I came here, it was with the intention of listening and learning, but also providing American leadership. And I think that the document that has been produced as well as the concrete actions that will follow reflect a range of our priorities...."

"We've got a global economy, and if we're taking actions in isolation in the United States, but those actions are contradicted overseas, then we're only going to be halfway effective... [We have had] a drastic reduction in US exports... and the contagion from the financial markets debilitating the economies elsewhere" is affecting other US companies that were looking more solid," he said.

Obama explained, "this is a collective document. But there's no doubt that each country has its own quirks and own particular issues... something that is non-negotiable for them. And what we tried to do as much as possible was to accommodate those issues in a way that didn't—did not hamper the effectiveness of the overall document..."

"That does not entirely solve the problem of toxic assets... And how each individual nation acts to deal with that is still going to be vitally important. How well we execute the respective stimulus programs around the world is going to be very important. The quicker they are... the more all of us will benefit."

"I think there has always been a spectrum of opinion about how unfettered the free market is.... [T]here have been some who believe in very fierce regulation and are very suspicious of globalization and there are others who think that... the market is always king.... [B]ut if anybody had been studying history they would have understood... that the market is the most effective mechanism for creating wealth... but that it goes off the rails sometimes; that if it's not regulated, if there are no thoughtful frameworks to channel the creative energy of the market, that it can end up in a very bad place."

"In terms of local politics, look, I'm the president of the United States. I'm not the president of China, I'm not the president of Japan, I'm not

> the president of the other participants here. And so I have a direct responsibility to my constituents to make their lives better.... That accounts for some of the questions here, about how concretely does me being here help them find a job, pay for their home, send their kids to college, live what we call the American Dream...."
>
> "[I]international polls seem to indicate that you're seeing people more hopeful about America's leadership."
>
> "I wouldn't be here if I didn't think that we had important things to contribute."
>
> "There's been a lot of comparison here about Bretton Woods.... But that's not the world we live in.... Europe is now rebuilt and a powerhouse.... China, India—these are all countries on the move. And that's good."
>
> "There were occasional comments... that [suggested] that this [crisis] started in America, or started on Wall Street... [W]e had a number of firms that took wild and unjustified risks... and it has taken an enormous toll on the US economy and has spread to the world economy."

It may be appreciated that Obama's answers to the journalists were basically addressed to his constituents. They express what the US president is thinking. Undoubtedly, he is much better than Bush and McCain, but his thinking is not geared to the real problems of today's world. The empire is much more powerful than he is or his good intentions.

The G-20 Summit announced in its final communiqué they will triple the resources for the International Monetary Fund to the figure of $750 billion; $500 billion for loans to countries most affected by the crisis and $250 billion for a new Special Drawing Rights (SDR) allocation.

Another $100 billion will be destined to reinforce the multilateral development banks.

On the other hand, they will provide $250 billion to reactivate world trade.

I should point out that these funds will be contributed by the European Union, Japan, China and other countries, as well as through the sales of part of the IMF gold reserves.

The British prime minister stated that a new international order is emerging and added that the old Washington consensus is over; he also said today's decisions will not immediately solve the crisis.

The French president claimed that he was "truly happy" about the summit results, considering that the measures adopted constitute the deepest reform of the financial system since 1945. He didn't have to walk out of the room.

The US Department of Labor reported that in March the number of people continuing to receive unemployment benefits increased to a new historic high of 5.73 million.

Obama spoke of Bretton Woods. At the end of World War II, the United States possessed 80 percent of the world's gold and its booming economy was intact. Bretton Woods granted it the privilege of issuing hard currency while the rest of the world was bankrupt.

The United States had both dollars and gold. The price of gold remained stable for more than 25 years until the US government, bankrupted by the imperialist Vietnam War, unilaterally suspended dollar conversion and proceeded to manipulate, at its whim, the economies of the rest of the world.

The crisis is indissolubly wed to the capitalist system of production and distribution. Its main paradigm, the United States, has suffered two great crises throughout its history that dealt harsh blows to its economy during periods of more than 20 years. This is the third crisis and from which recovery will be very slow. Europe knows this because of its own bitter experience.

The US transnational companies acquired holdings throughout the world by virtue of Bretton Woods. They would pay with gold and with paper money; today they buy them with paper money or "junk money" as the Chinese like to call it. Furthermore, the United States has the rare privilege of veto power in the International Monetary Fund. Not one word has been uttered in London that would challenge this US privilege. The next crisis will happen much sooner and will be much more serious than Obama and several of his main G-7 allies could ever imagine. Crises are not resolved by either administrative or technical measures, because they are systemic and each time they affect the economy and globalization of the planet.

Not everybody was swept up in the euphoria in London.

An AFP cable reported that on Thursday Navi Pillay, the UN High Commissioner for Human Rights, criticized the G-20 Summit, complaining that the demonstrators and the poorest countries had been excluded: "As High Commissioner for Human Rights I would say that financial policy should not be limited to the banks, but it should be dedicated to human beings whose concerns ought to be at the center of the debates. The G-20 Summit should immediately center its attention on the concerns of workers and of poor peasants."

Numerous demonstrations took place in London to protest against the summit.

Another cable reported that Jean Ping, president of the African Union Commission, commented on the summit: "We are not asking countries to put their hands in their pockets and give us money because they've promised, promised, promised and done nothing."

While supposed lifesaving measures were being adopted in London, the specter of climate change arose on the very day the final G-20 agreement was passed, a tragedy more serious than the economic crisis.

An AFP cable read: "According to a new scientific study, around 80 percent of the Arctic polar ice cap could disappear by a date as soon as the year 2040, instead of staying around until 2100 as it had been estimated earlier."

"At that time, the surface of the Arctic ocean covered by ice at the end of the summer might not exceed a million square kilometers, as compared to 4.6 million square kilometers today." This report was drawn up with data provided by scientists from Washington State University and the US National Oceanic and Atmospheric Administration in a joint study. According to this study, the Arctic polar ice cap suffered a spectacular reduction in size at the end of the summers of 2007 and 2008, when the ice surface had reached 4.3 and 4.7 million square kilometers, respectively.

The applied models allow for a prediction of a practically iceless Arctic in 32 years. According to the scientists, previous models foresaw this scenario happening by the end of the 21st century. An enormous mass of water is accumulated there in the thick polar ice cap at a great height.

Granma repeated this news in today's edition.

On April 1, I wrote about both problems: the international financial crisis and climate change. The purpose here is not to sow discouragement but to build awareness. There is nothing worse than ignorance. No matter how fantastic the sports classics are, we should not sit back and ignore such pressing issues as the economy, the climate and science. I am a sports fan like anyone else, but human beings do not live by bread alone.

April 3, 2009

Walking on Solid Ground

On April 2, while the G-20 Summit was held in London, the well-known journalist of the influential *Washington Post*, Karen DeYoung, wrote: "Senator Richard G. Lugar called on President Obama to appoint a special envoy to initiate direct talks with [Cuba's] communist government."

> "The nearly 50-year-old economic embargo against Cuba, Lugar (R-Ind.) said,... puts the United States at odds with the views of the rest of Latin America, the European Union and the United Nations, and 'undermines our broader security and political interests in the Western Hemisphere.'
>
> "The April 17-19 Summit of the Americas in Trinidad and Tobago would present a 'unique opportunity for you to build a more hospitable climate to advance US interests in the region through a change in our posture regarding Cuba policy.'
>
> "Lugar, the ranking Republican on the Senate Foreign Relations Committee… is in the forefront of a broad movement advocating a new policy that includes the US Chamber of Commerce and other business groups, a number of state governments and human rights groups. A bipartisan majority of Congress has repeatedly voted to ease restrictions on travel and other contact with Cuba, although the measures died after threatened presidential vetoes during the Bush administration.
>
> "Lugar is a co-sponsor of a bipartisan bill introduced in the Senate this week that would end all restrictions on travel to Cuba except in cases of war or direct threats to health or safety.
>
> "Lugar said the appointment of an envoy and initiation of direct talks on subjects such as migration and drug interdiction would 'serve vital

> US security interests... and could ultimately create the conditions for meaningful discussion of more contentious subjects'."

Karen's article expresses no doubt that the Indiana senator is walking on solid ground. His starting point is not a philanthropic position. As she states, he is working with "the US Chamber of Commerce and other business groups, a number of state governments and human rights groups."

I am certain Richard G. Lugar doesn't fear the absurdity of being described as soft or pro-socialist.

If President Barack Obama travels the world asserting, as he has in his own country, that it is necessary to invest the sums needed to pull it out of the financial crisis, to guarantee the homes where countless families live, to guarantee jobs for US workers who are becoming unemployed in their millions, to establish health services and quality education for all citizens, how can he reconcile all this with blockade measures in order to impose his will over a country like Cuba?

Today drugs are one of the most serious problems in this hemisphere and in Europe. In the war against drug trafficking and organized crime, stimulated by the enormous US market, Latin American countries are now losing almost 10,000 people men each year, more than twice the number lost by the United States in the Iraq war. The number grows and the problem is very far from being resolved.

Such a phenomenon does not exist in Cuba, a close neighboring country to the United States. On this thorny subject, and in the war against illegal migration, the US and Cuban coast guard services have been cooperating for many years. On the other hand, no American has ever died as the result of terrorist actions coming from our country, because such activities would not be tolerated.

The Cuban revolution, which has not been destroyed either by the blockade or the dirty war, is based on ethical and political principles; that is the reason why it has been able to resist.

My aim here is not to exhaust this subject. Far from it; in this "Reflection" I am leaving aside the damage inflicted on our country by the US's arrogant attitude toward Cuba.

Those who are capable of calmly analyzing events, as in the case of the senator from Indiana, make an irrefutable argument: The US measures against Cuba, over almost half a century, are a total failure.

There is no need to emphasize what Cuba has always said: We do not fear dialogue with the United States. Nor do we need the confrontation to exist as some foolish people think. We exist precisely because we believe in our ideas and we have never feared dialogue with our adversaries. It is the only way to secure friendship and peace among peoples.

April 5, 2009

The Visit of Seven Members of the US Congress

An important US political delegation is visiting us right now. Its members belong to the Congressional Black Caucus (CBC) which, in practice, acts as the most progressive wing within the Democratic Party.

The Congressional Black Caucus was founded in January 1969 by the 12 African-American legislators who belonged to the US Congress at that time. During the first 50 years of the 20th century only four African Americans were elected to Congress.

At present, as a result of the struggles they have waged, the CBC has 42 members. Several of its representatives have maintained very active and constructive positions on issues related to Cuba.

The first caucus delegation to visit us came to Cuba in February 1999 and was led by Maxine Waters; the second came in January, 2000.

Influential members of that Congressional group publicly expressed their positions and carried out other positive actions during the battle for the return of the child Elián [González] to his homeland.

In May 2000, another Caucus delegation visited us. It was led by James Clyburn, from North Carolina, who was then its main leader, and included Bennie Thompson, from Mississippi, and Gregory Meeks, from New York. These congressmen were the first to hear from me about Cuba's readiness to grant a number of scholarships to low-income youth, who were to be selected by the Congressional Black Caucus, so that they could come to Cuba and study medicine. We made a similar offer to Pastors for Peace, which is led by Reverend Lucius Walker, who sent the first students to the Latin American Medical School (ELAM).

When the Bush administration adopted anti-Cuba measures and actions against travel and the presence in Cuba of people under US jurisdiction became more severe, the Black Caucus legislators spoke to Secretary of State Colin Powell and managed to secure a license that legally allowed American youth to continue the medical studies, which they had already commenced in Cuba.

Powell, a military chief of great authority and prestige, could have been the first black president of the United States, but he refused to be nominated out of respect for his family which, remembering the assassination of Martin Luther King, Jr., firmly opposed his nomination.

The Black Caucus delegation visiting Cuba this time is led by Barbara Lee, representative from California. She first came to Cuba accompanying the then black Congressman Ronald Dellums. She was his assistant and afterwards occupied his seat when he retired. On that occasion I had the honor of meeting her personally and admire her combative spirit and capacity for struggle.

The group she is leading right now is made up of seven members of Congress. The other members of the delegation are: Melvin Luther Watt, from North Carolina; Michael Makoto Honda, from California; Laura Richardson, also from California; Bobby Rush, from Illinois; Marcia L. Fudge, from Ohio; and Emanuel Cleaver II, from Missouri.

Patrice Willoughby, executive assistant of the Congressional Black Caucus, plus four military personnel from the Congressional Liaison Office, under the orders of Lt. Col. Daniel Wolf, are accompanying the delegation.

I highly appreciate the gesture of this group of lawmakers. They have been strictly complying with the program they asked for. Martin Luther King's aureole accompanies them. Our press has given a broad coverage to their visit. They have been exceptional witnesses to the respect with which we always welcome North Americans to our homeland. They have seen hatred on no one's face, and possibly they admire the total absence of illiterate people or children shining shoes on the streets. The swarms of children, teenagers and youth attending schools and universities; the day-care centers, senior citizens homes, hospitals and polyclinics run by highly skilled medical staff offering assistance to all citizens will not have escaped the notice of any critical eye. In the midst of this international economic crisis there are no citizens queuing up to apply for a job. People move about streets in an active and almost always happy manner, unlike the stereotype image of Cuba that is usually portrayed abroad.

Our homeland is showing that a small Third World country, which has been besieged, attacked and blockaded for decades, can abide its poverty with dignity. Many citizens in the richest nation of the world do not receive the same treatment, and a considerable number of them do not even vote. However, that right is exercised quite often by more than 90 percent of our population, which knows how to read and write and has acquired a not-inconsiderable level of culture and political knowledge.

Among the visitors there are opinions which are shared by all; others are personal points of view. In general, they believe that 68 percent of US public opinion favors a change in the policy toward Cuba.

One of them expressed the view that it was necessary to take advantage of this historic moment, when the presence of a black president in the White House coincides with current opinion that favors the normalization of relations.

When [Cuban National Assembly president Ricardo] Alarcón explained that removing Cuba from the list of terrorist states—where it has been arbitrarily included—was a moral duty, he recalled that both Nelson Mandela and the African National Congress had been labeled as terrorists by the US Congress.

Another member of the delegation thanked the Cuban authorities and the presidency of the Black Caucus for promoting the trip and arranging for this type of exchange.

Another representative explained Obama's great significance for the United States and the need for him to be re-elected. He said the president believes himself a political leader who should govern for all social sectors of the country. Nevertheless, he said he was sure that Obama will change the policy toward Cuba, but Cuba should also help him.

A fourth member of the caucus said that despite Obama's electoral victory, US society continues to be racist. He added that Obama represented the only opportunity the nation had to move on and leave behind all the wrongs perpetuated by former governments. He said the president cannot go beyond liberalizing travel and allowing remittances by Cuban Americans, because proclaiming the lifting of the blockade or the full normalization of bilateral relations could mean he would not be re-elected. Besides, he reaffirmed that the anti-Cuba right wing still has enough power to corner him and prevent his re-election.

Finally, another lawmaker at the Ministry of Foreign Affairs said frankly the United States should not lose the opportunity of recognizing its Cuba policy has been an absolute failure. He added that his government should apologize to Cuba for all these years of hostility and for the blockade, because only then will we be in a position to move on together toward the solution of the bilateral dispute. He pointed out that, from his position, he would do whatever is possible to eliminate the blockade.

During their visit to the Biotechnology and Genetic Engineering Center, one of them, expressing the feelings of the rest, described the excellent results Cuba has achieved in biotechnology, and said that, at this moment, the political atmosphere was favorable to building bridges of understanding and communication between the scientific communities of our respective countries. He recommended that we should be careful and patent everything, according to the international intellectual property standards, to prevent our being robbed of the efforts that led to such a wonderful work.

All of them expressed how greatly impressed they were during the visit to the center, where the minister of science, technology and the environment, together with the directors of several scientific institutions, explained the work carried out by our country in that field.

The main activity of April 4, a day marking the 41st anniversary of the death of the human rights martyr, was the visit to the park in Cuba's capital named after Martin Luther King, Jr., where there is a black-veined dark green marble monolith, bearing the bronze embossed image of the great black fighter who was assassinated by a racist. Barbara Lee, Laura Richardson, Emanuel Cleaver II and Bobby Rush took the floor at the gathering. The four of them publicly emphasized the positive impact of the meetings they had held.

Yesterday (Sunday) at 1:20 p.m., Congresswoman Barbara Lee arrived at the Ebenezer Church of the Martin Luther King Center, where she was welcomed by Raúl Suárez and other executives of Cuba's National Council of Churches. Also present were Alarcón and other officials from the Ministry of Foreign Affairs.

Earlier Barbara Lee had visited two other churches in Vedado. She addressed the congregation; she reiterated some of her previous public statements and expressed her intention to work with the administration to promote a change of policy toward Cuba and to reactivate exchanges between the churches of both countries.

I have summarized here as far as possible the exchanges that took place. I have been careful enough not to disclose the names of those who made certain statements, because I do not know whether they want them publicized.

I only wanted to offer some essential elements so that our people have as much information as possible on the sensitive subject of relations between Cuba and the United States under Obama's presidency and the visit of the Black Caucus delegation to Cuba.

April 6, 2009

Contradictions in US Foreign Policy

After the G-20 Summit that attracted world attention, the press agencies continued to broadcast reports about the feverish activity of the man who had starred in London, Barack Obama, the new president of the United States, who has now marked the first 100 days of his administration under the close scrutiny of those who follow international politics. As punctual as a digital watch, he travels from one place to the next, meeting with political leaders, commemorating anniversaries, receiving honors, visiting cities, holding press conferences, announcing plans, delivering messages and making speeches.

With the supersonic G-20 Summit barely concluded, he leaves for Strasbourg, France, on the German border. He meets there on April 3 with [President] Sarkozy who was happy about not having had to leave the G-20 table in London. They discuss numerous problems concerning Iran, Afghanistan, Russia, the Near East and they promise to work "hand in hand" to build a new world. "I am convinced that the United States, Russia and Europe are interested in preventing Iran from having nuclear weapons. In many instances we have common interests with Russia, but we also have differences of opinion on key issues," he states.

It is announced that both Obama and Sarkozy will participate with 26 other countries in the NATO summit to begin that afternoon in the German town of Baden-Baden and would conclude the following day in Strasbourg.

Before leaving, he states, "Europe should not let the United States bear this burden alone because this is a problem concerning both and a joint effort is necessary.... We do not seek to be chiefs in Europe; we are seeking to be partners with Europe."

He leaves Strasbourg en route to the town of Baden-Baden to meet with German Chancellor Angela Merkel before a dinner with the 26 NATO heads of states and governments, plus those of Croatia and Albania who are applying for membership. The summit will serve as the opening for the 60th anniversary celebrations of the military organization. There they intend to analyze relations with Russia that "reached their lowest point in the past month of August after the Russia-Georgia war."

Another objective was discussion to renew the alliance's 1999 concept of strategic action to adjust it to the new threats.

Discussion of the Afghanistan and Kosovo situation would follow.

On April 3 in Strasbourg, Obama meets with more than 3,000 young French and Germans and he delivers a short speech which, because of its audacity, will certainly be a talking point for some time to come.

"I have come to Europe this week to renew our alliance. The United States is changing but it cannot only be America that is changing," he said, and then announced the substance of the speech he will be making in Prague about nuclear proliferation, asserting that his aim is "a world without nuclear weapons."

Later he added, "Even now that the Cold War has ended the expansion of nuclear weapons or the theft of nuclear material could bring destruction to any city on the planet."

The growing concern in the world about the enormous destructive and annihilating power of those weapons is unquestionable; it unites the concerns of other states and US society itself about the risks of nuclear sabotage. This is what Obama means with his statement "the theft of nuclear material could bring destruction to any city on the planet."

On April 4, in a speech at the NATO summit, Obama welcomed Croatia and Albania to the heart of that military organization, thus bringing to 28 the number of members. The president of the United States stressed that 140 Albanian and 296 Croatian soldiers have served in Afghanistan and remarked he thought "both will be steadfast contributors to the alliance."

The contradictory ways in which the US president expresses his ideas are evident when he says: "The doors of the alliance will continue to be open to other countries who comply with NATO standards and who can make a significant contribution to the security of the alliance."

The EFE news agency explains: "Russia reveals itself to be highly critical of NATO expansion toward the east, and in particular toward the former Soviet republics that it considers to be its natural sphere of influence."

"Last year at its April summit in Bucharest, the alliance promised an eventual path to the admission of the Ukraine and Georgia supported by Obama's predecessor George W. Bush," the cable reminds us.

Can there be any doubt that NATO is a warlike and aggressive organization, one that threatens not only Russia but also other countries elsewhere in the world? Could the Guantánamo torture center have been created and maintained without the cooperation of numerous NATO countries?

Yet again, the audacity and the contradictions are expressed at the first summit of the US president with the European Union in Prague where he promised "to lead efforts for a world without nuclear weapons."

"We cannot succeed in this endeavor alone, but we can lead it," he said.

He specifically stated he hoped to achieve a speedy end to nuclear testing and confirmed his hope of seeking Senate approval for the Comprehensive Test Ban Treaty.

"I also advocate a world summit meeting on nuclear security to be held next year," the cables report.

There is also a report that "Obama was woken up to be informed of the launching of a North Korean rocket that apparently flew over Japan. He requested that the UN Security Council respond strongly to the provocation in an emergency meeting held that very same Sunday."

On March 12, the Peoples' Republic of Korea had announced that between April 4 and 8 it would be launching a communications satellite as part of a peaceful space program. This was known when Obama spoke in Strasbourg to the French and German youth.

After he was informed in Prague [about the North Korean rocket], he drew up a statement that said: "Rules must be binding. Violations must be punished. Words must mean something."

Launching a rocket that will facilitate communications, testing technology or taking a tourist on a trip are not crimes unless they are done by the Peoples' Republic of Korea that does not belong to the club of the most powerful and those who have the resources to apply such sophisticated technology. Japan took advantage of the opportunity to adjust its anti-satellite missiles and to improve its defense without anybody questioning that right.

I think it was an overreaction to wake up Obama in the early morning hours.

Before leaving Prague, at a gathering of 30,000 people, Obama said, "To say that nuclear weapons are inevitable is like saying that the use of nuclear weapons is inevitable. Humanity must once again become master of its own destiny." This is a very strong assertion. However, he later added that the space shield the United States projects for European territory is a program in response to the Iranian nuclear menace. Such a statement is not consistent with the truth and I do not understand why he repeated it.

Russia rejects the plan for the space shield and considers it to be expansionist and, therefore, demands its cancellation.

During the night of Sunday April 5, Obama arrived in Turkey. After meeting on Monday with Turkish leaders in Ankara, the capital of that Euro-Asian nation, and delivering a speech in parliament, he announced he would be traveling to Istanbul to attend the second forum of the Alliance of Civilizations.

In Prague he had promised to support Turkey's admittance into the European Union, something which is opposed by France, Germany and others. In Ankara, he again asked for Turkish admission to the European Union, but pointed out that Turkey should make efforts to reinforce its democracy.

The first thing he did upon arrival in that country was to pay tribute to Mustafa Kemal Ataturk, the founder of the Turkish Republic. "We will be respectful even though we may not agree," he told parliament—another profound phrase.

"The United States is not, nor will it be, at war with Islam," he said. Thousands of Turks had taken to the streets to protest US policies.

The president of the United States ended his visit on April 7 at 2:20 Istanbul time, Turkey's main city, after a tiring 8-day tour.

His last meeting was with the students. He made a plea to the young people to lay bridges between Islam and the West. As EFE reported, he urged Muslims to ignore the "caricatures" that depict Americans as ignorant or insensitive and he assured them that "that is not the country he loves."

The events described reflect the complexity of the tasks Obama bears on his shoulders. He had frankly declared: "In four or eight years it will be said whether I have pursued the same policies or if things have changed."

Even though he was a messenger relaying mixed signals, his obvious good health and agile mind operating like a working machine allowed the black president to carry out his first foreign visit with unquestionable political results.

He certainly does not resemble his predecessor in the least.

April 8, 2009

Not a Word About the Blockade

The US administration announced through CNN that Obama would be visiting Mexico this week, in the first part of a trip that will take him to Port of Spain, Trinidad and Tobago, where he will take part in the Summit of the Americas in four days' time. He has announced the removal of some hateful restrictions imposed by Bush on Cubans living in the United States regarding their visits to relatives in Cuba. When questions were raised about whether such prerogatives extended to other US citizens, the response was that the latter are not authorized to travel to Cuba.

Not a word was said about the harshest of measures: the blockade. This is the way a truly genocidal measure is piously referred to, one whose damage cannot be calculated only on the basis of its economic effects, for it constantly takes human lives and brings painful suffering to our people.

Much diagnostic equipment and essential medicines that are made in Europe, Japan or any other country are not available to Cuban patients if they contain US components or software. The US companies producing goods or offering services anywhere in the world have to apply these restrictions to Cuba, since they are extraterritorial measures.

An influential Republican senator, Richard Lugar, and others from his same party in Congress, as well as a significant number of his Democratic peers, favor the removal of the blockade. The conditions exist for Obama to use his talents in a constructive policy that could put an end to one that has failed for almost half a century.

On the other hand, our country, which has resisted and is willing to resist whatever it takes, neither blames Obama for the atrocities of other US administrations nor doubts his sincerity and his wish to change US policy and its image. We understand he waged a very difficult battle to be elected, despite centuries-old prejudice.

Taking note of this reality, the president of the Cuban Council of State has expressed his willingness to have a dialogue with Obama and to normalize relations with the United States, on the basis of the strictest respect for the sovereignty of our country.

At 2:30 p.m., the head of the Interests Section of Cuba in Washington, Jorge Bolaños, was summoned to the State Department by Deputy Secretary of State Thomas Shannon. He said nothing different from what had been reported on CNN.

At 3:15 p.m. a lengthy press conference was held. The substance of what was said there is reflected in the words of Dan Restrepo, presidential advisor for Latin America.

He said today President Obama had ordered certain measures, certain steps, to reach out to the Cuban people in support of their wishes to live with respect for human rights and to determine their own destiny and that of the country.

He added that the president had instructed the secretaries of state, commerce and treasury to undertake the necessary actions to remove all restrictions preventing people to visit their relatives on the island and sending remittances. He also said the president had issued instructions for steps to be taken allowing the free flow of information in Cuba, and between those living in Cuba and the rest of the world, and to facilitate the delivery of humanitarian resources directly to the Cuban people.

He also said that, with these measures aimed at closing the gap that divides Cuban families and promoting the free flow of information and humanitarian assistance to the Cuban people, President Obama was making an effort to fulfill the objectives he set out during his campaign and since taking office.

Finally, he indicated that all those who believe in basic democratic values hope for a Cuba where the human, political, economic and basic rights of the entire people are respected. And he added that President Obama feels that these measures will help to make this objective a reality. The president, he said, encourages everyone who shares these wishes to continue to steadfastly support the Cuban people.

At the end of the press conference, the advisor candidly confessed that "all of this is for Cuba's freedom."

Cuba does not applaud the ill-named Summits of the Americas, where our nations do not debate on equal footing. If they had any purpose, it would be to make a critical analysis of the policies that divide our peoples, plunder our resources and hinder our development.

Now, the only thing left is for Obama to try to persuade all the Latin American presidents attending the conference that the blockade is inoffensive.

Cuba has resisted and will continue to resist; it will never beg for alms. It will go forward holding its head high, cooperating with the fraternal peoples of Latin America and the Caribbean, with or without Summits of the Americas and whether or not the president of the United States is Obama, a man or a woman, a black or a white citizen.

April 13, 2009

Military Men with Correct Opinions

Who knows how many people in the United States write to Obama and how many different issues he is presented with. It's clear he cannot read all the letters and deal with everything because he wouldn't be able to achieve this in a 24-hour day or a 365-day year. What is certain is that his advisors, backed up by their computers, electronic equipment and cell phones, answer all the letters. Their contents are recorded and there are pre-written answers supported by the many statements made by the president during his election campaign.

Anyway, these letters have an influence and bearing upon US policy since we are not dealing, in this case, with a corrupt, lying and ignorant politician as his predecessor was, a man who hated the social advances made by the New Deal.

For that reason I focused on a news report published yesterday (April 14) originating from Washington, provided by the DPA news agency.

It stated that a group of high-ranking retired US military officials were urging President Barack Obama to "support and sign" a law to end the travel ban to Cuba for all US citizens, arguing that the embargo against the island serves no political purpose or affects Washington's security.

In a letter released today in Washington, the 12 high-ranking retired officers, among them the "drug czar" during the Clinton administration, Barry McCaffrey, and Colin Powell's former chief of staff, Lawrence B. Wilkerson, warn that the embargo has caused "a significant diplomatic movement against US policy."

"As military professionals, we understand that the interests of America are best served when the United States is able to attract the support of other nations to our cause," the military men insist in the letter sent to Obama on Monday, the same day the US president announced the end of the travel restrictions and remittances for Cuban Americans, but not for all US citizens as progressive sectors are demanding.

In the opinion of these military men, the Law on Freedom of Travel to Cuba presented before the House of Representatives by the Democrat Bill Delahunt "is an important first step toward the lifting of the embargo."

They add that this kind of policy is "more likely to bring change to Cuba" and also for changing Washington's international image. "[A]round the world, leaders are calling for a real policy shift that delivers on the hope you [Obama] inspired in your campaign," they argue, adding that "Cuba offers the lowest-hanging fruit for such a shift and would be a move that would register deeply in the minds of our partners and competitors around the world."

Placed as it was among 315 pages of cables, this news item would appear to be somewhat insignificant. However it deals with the crux of the problem that motivated my four "Reflections" in less than 24 hours concerning the Summit of the Americas that will be starting within 48 hours.

In the United States, wars are unleashed by politicians but they must be fought by soldiers.

The young and untried Kennedy decreed the blockade [against Cuba] and the Bay of Pigs invasion, organized by Eisenhower and by Nixon who knew less about war than he did. An unexpected twist of fate led him to new and unwise decisions that led to the October Missile Crisis from which he nevertheless emerged gracefully. But he remained traumatized by the prospect of a nuclear war that hovered at his elbow, as the French journalist Jean Daniel told me. "He is a thinking machine," was how Daniel praised the president who had greatly impressed him.

Later, enthused over the Green Berets, he dispatched them to Vietnam where the United States was supporting the restoration of the French colonial empire. Another politician, Lyndon Johnson, carried that war to its final consequences. In that inglorious adventure, more than 50,000 soldiers lost their lives, the United States squandered no less than $500 billion when the value of the dollar in gold fell 20 times, killed millions of Vietnamese and expanded the solidarity with that poor Third World country. Conscripts had to be replaced with professional soldiers, separating the people from military training and thus weakening the nation.

A third politician, George W. Bush, protected by his father, carried out the genocidal Iraqi war that hastened the economic crisis, making it more serious and profound. Its cost in economic terms is trillions of dollars, with a public debt that will fall upon new generations of Americans, in a world that is convulsed and full of risks.

Those who affirm that the embargo affects the security interests of the United States, are they right or not?

Those who wrote the letter are not appealing for the use of weapons, but to a war of ideas, something that is the diametrical opposite of what was done by the politicians.

In general, the US military men who defend the economic, political and social system of the United States have privileges and are very well paid, but they are concerned about not taking participating in the theft of public funds, something that would lead them into disrepute and undermine the authority of their military endeavors.

They do not believe Cuba constitutes a threat to the security of the United States, as we have been portrayed to US public opinion. It has been the various governments of that country which transformed the Guantánamo base into a refuge for counter-revolutionaries or emigrants. Worse than all this, they transformed it into a torture center that has made them famous as a symbol of the most brutal negation of human rights.

The military men also know that our country is a model for the fight against drug trafficking and that terrorist actions have never been allowed against the people of the United States from our territory.

As the Black Caucus delegation from the US Congress was able to discover, including Cuba on the list of terrorist countries is the most dishonest thing that has ever been done.

We give thanks to those who wrote the letter to Obama, just as we thank senators Lugar and Delahunt, the Black Caucus and other influential members of Congress.

We do not fear dialogue; we do not need to invent enemies; we do not fear the debate of ideas; we hold firmly to our convictions and we have known how to defend and continue defending our homeland.

With the fabulous advances of technology, war has become one of the most complex sciences. This is something the US military men understand. They know it is not a matter of issuing orders along the lines of old wars. Nowadays, one will possibly never see the adversary's face; they can be thousands of kilometers away; the deadliest weapons are fired by computer programs. Human beings hardly participate. Decisions are coolly calculated in advance.

I have met several of these retired military men, who dedicate themselves to the study of military science and warfare. They express no hatred or dislike of the small country that has struggled and resisted, faced with such a powerful neighbor.

These days there is a World Security Institute in the United States; our country maintains contact with it and carries out academic exchanges. Fifteen years ago there was the Center for Defense Information (CDI); they made a first visit to Cuba at the end of June in 1993. Between that date and November 19, 2004, nine visits were made to Cuba.

Until 1999, the delegations were mainly made up of retired military officials. In the October 1999 visit, the composition of the delegates began to change, and the military had less of a presence. From the fifth visit, all the delegations were led by the prestigious researcher Bruce Blair, an expert in security policy and specializing in nuclear control and command forces. He is a consulting professor at the universities of Yale and Princeton and has published many books and hundreds of articles on the subject.

This was how I met military men who had played important roles in the US armed forces. We did not always agree with their point of view, but they were always pleasant. We had extensive exchanges about the historical events in which they had participated. Visits continued in 2006, but I had the accident in Santa Clara and later on I became seriously ill.

Among the 12 retired soldiers who signed the letter to Obama, one of them had taken part in those meetings. I learned in our last meeting, they said frankly that the military had no intention of militarily attacking Cuba; that there was a new political situation in the United States arising from the administration's weakness on account of its disaster in Iraq.

For the compañeros who met with the North Americans it was evident that they felt they were being poorly led and they were embarrassed by what was happening, even though nobody could provide guarantees about [President Bush's] adventurous policy that he maintained until his last day in office. That meeting took place in March of 2007, 14 months ago.

Bruce Blair must know much more than I about this thorny subject. I was always impressed by his brave and transparent conduct.

I didn't want this information to remain in the archives waiting for a time when it would no longer be of interest to anyone.

April 15, 2009

Obama and the Blockade

Yesterday I referred to what was comical about the Port of Spain Declaration of Commitment [from the Summit of the Americas].

Today I could refer to what is tragic about it. I hope our friends take no offense in this. There were some differences between the draft we received, which was going to be submitted by the hosts of the summit, and the final document that was published. In all the last-minute haste, there was hardly any time for anything. Some items had been discussed at long meetings held some weeks prior to the summit. At the very last moment, proposals such as the one submitted by Bolivia complicated the whole picture even more. The Bolivian proposal was included as a note in the document and stated that Bolivia considered the implementation of policies and cooperation schemes aimed at expanding the use of bio-fuels in the western hemisphere could affect and have an impact on the availability of foodstuffs, increase food prices, deforestation, the displacement of populations as a result of the demand for land, and that consequently this could exacerbate the food crisis. This would directly affect low-income people and, most of all, the poorest economies among developing countries. The note added that, while recognizing the need to look for and resort to environmentally friendly alternative sources of energy, such as geothermal, solar and wind, and small- and medium-sized hydro-electric power generators, the Bolivian government advocates an alternative approach, based on the possibility of living well and in harmony with nature, in order to develop public policies aimed at the promotion of safe alternative energies that ensure the preservation of the planet, our "mother earth."

When analyzing this note submitted by Bolivia, it should be remembered that the United States and Brazil are the two biggest producers of bio-fuels in the world, something opposed by an increasing number of people on the planet, whose resistance has been growing since the dark days of George Bush.

Obama's advisors published on the Internet their version—in English—of the interview the US president granted to some journalists in Port of Spain. At one point, he asserted that there was something he found interesting—adding that he had known about it generally but that he found it interesting to learn more details. This was listening to these leaders who, when speaking about Cuba, referred specifically to the thousands of doctors Cuba is sending throughout the region, and learning how much these countries depended on these doctors. He said this reminded them in the United States of the fact that if their only interaction with many of these [Latin American] countries was the war on drugs, that if the only interaction was of a military character, then it was possible that the United States would not be developing connections that, with time, would enhance its influence with a positive effect when it was necessary to advance its interests in the region.

He said he thought that was the reason why it was so important—for the sake of their interaction, not only here in this hemisphere, but in the whole world—to recognize that US military power was just part of its power, and that it had to resort to diplomacy and development aid in a more intelligent way, so that people could see concrete and practical improvements in the life of ordinary citizens, based on the foreign policy of the United States.

Jake, one of the journalists, thanked the president and added that in Port of Spain the president had listened to many Latin American leaders who want the United States to lift the embargo against Cuba. The journalist reminded the president he had said it was important and should not be eliminated, but added that in 2004 the president had actually supported lifting the embargo. He reminded the president he had said the embargo had not managed to raise the standard of living, that it had squeezed the innocent, and that it was high time for the United States to recognize that this particular policy had failed. The journalist asked what had made the president change his mind about the embargo.

The president responded that 2004 seemed to be "thousands of years ago," and wondered what he himself was doing in that year.

The journalist reminded him he was running for the Senate at that time. The president remarked it was a sign of progress that Raúl Castro had said his government was ready to talk with the US government not only about the lifting of the embargo but also about other issues, namely, human rights and political prisoners. He said there were some things the Cuban government could do. He added that Cuba could release the political prisoners, reduce the surcharge imposed on remittances, which would match the new US government policy regarding remittances from Cuban-American families. He explained Cuba applies a very high surcharge from which it is exacting significant profits. He added that this would be an example of cooperation where both governments would be working to help Cuban families and improve living standards in Cuba.

There is no doubt the president misinterpreted Raúl's statements. When the Cuban president said he was ready to discuss any topic with the US president, he meant he was not afraid of addressing any issue. That shows his courage and confidence in the principles of the revolution. No one should be astonished that Raúl spoke about pardoning those who were convicted in March 2003 and sending them all to the United States, should that country be willing to release the five Cuban anti-terrorism heroes. The convicts, as was the case with the Bay of Pigs mercenaries, act in the service of a foreign power that threatens and blockades our homeland.

Besides, the assertion that Cuba imposes a very high surcharge and obtains significant profits [from remittances] is an attempt by the president's advisors to cause trouble and sow division among Cubans. Every country charges a certain amount for all hard currency transfers. If these are in dollars, all the more reason we have to do it, because that is the currency of the country that blockades us. Not all Cubans have relatives abroad who can send them remittances. Redistributing a relatively small part of this to benefit those more in need of food, medicines and other goods is absolutely fair. Our homeland does not have the privilege of converting the money minted by the state into hard currency—something the Chinese call "junk money"—which, as I have explained on several occasions, has been one of the causes of the present economic crisis. What money is the United States using to bail out its banks and multinationals, while plunging future generations of Americans into indebtedness? Would Obama be ready to discuss those issues?

[Nicaraguan President] Daniel Ortega stated it very clearly when he remembered his first conversation with Carter, which today I will repeat: "I had the opportunity to meet with President Carter," he said, "and when he told me that now, after the Somoza dictatorship had been ousted, and the Nicaraguan people had defeated the Somoza dictatorship, it was high time for Nicaragua 'to change,' I responded, 'No, Nicaragua does not need to change; you are the ones who need to change. Nicaragua has never invaded the United States. Nicaragua has never mined US ports. Nicaragua has never launched a single stone against the US nation. Nicaragua has not imposed any government on the United States. You are the ones who need to change, not the Nicaraguans'."

At the press conference, as well as in the final meetings of the summit, Obama appeared self-satisfied. Such an attitude by the US president was consistent with the abject position adopted by some Latin American leaders. Some days ago I commented that whatever was said and done at the summit will come out anyway.

When the US president said, in answer to Jake, that thousands of years had elapsed since 2004, he was being superficial. Should we wait for so many years before the blockade is lifted? He did not impose it, but he has embraced it just as much as the previous ten US presidents did. Should he continue down that same path, we predict he will face a certain fiasco, just as all his predecessors did. That is not the dream entertained by Martin Luther King, Jr., whose role in the struggle for human rights will always illuminate the US people's path.

We are living in a new era. Change is unavoidable. Leaders only pass through; the peoples prevail. There is no need to wait for thousands of years to pass; only eight years will be enough until a new US president—who will no doubt be less intelligent, less promising and less admired internationally than Barack Obama—riding in a better armored car, or in a more modern helicopter, or in a more sophisticated plane, occupies that inglorious position.

Tomorrow we expect more news about the summit.

April 21, 2009

Obama's Speech in Cairo

On Thursday June 4, at the Islamic University of Al-Azhar in Cairo, Obama gave a speech of special interest to those of us who are closely following his political actions given the enormous might of the superpower he leads. I will cite his own words to indicate what I think are the basic ideas he expressed, thus summarizing his speech to save time. We need to know not only that he spoke but also what he said.

> "We meet at a time of great tension between the United Status and Muslims around the world...
>
> "The relationship between Islam and the West includes centuries of coexistence and cooperation, but also conflict and religious wars....
>
> "More recently, tension has been fed by colonialism that denied rights and opportunities to many Muslims, and a Cold War in which Muslim-majority countries were too often treated as proxies without regard to their own aspirations....
>
> "Violent extremists have exploited these tensions...
>
> "[This] has led some in my country to view Islam as inevitably hostile not only to America and Western countries, but also to human rights....
>
> "I have come here to seek a new beginning between the United States and Muslims around the world; one based upon mutual interest and mutual respect...
>
> "...they overlap, and share common principles—principles of justice and progress; tolerance and the dignity of all human beings....
>
> "No single speech can eradicate years of mistrust, nor can I answer in the time that I have all the complex questions that brought us to this point....

"As the Holy Koran tells us, 'Be conscious of God and speak always the truth.'…

"I'm a Christian, but my father came from a Kenyan family that includes generations of Muslims. As a boy, I spent several years in Indonesia and heard the call of the azaan at the break of dawn and at the fall of dusk. As a young man, I worked in Chicago communities where many found dignity and peace in their Muslim faith….

"It was Islam—at places like Al-Azhar University—that carried the light of learning through so many centuries, paving the way for Europe's Renaissance and Enlightenment….

"…And since our founding, American Muslims have enriched the United States. They have fought in our wars, they have served in government, stood for civil rights…

"And I consider it part of my responsibility as president of the United States to fight against negative stereotypes of Islam wherever they appear….

"America is not the crude stereotype of a self-interested empire….

"The dream of opportunity for all people has not come true for everyone in America…

"Words alone cannot meet the needs of our people.

"When a new type of flu infects one human being, all are at risk. When one nation pursues a nuclear weapon, the risk of nuclear attack rises for all nations….

"[A]ny world order that elevates one nation or group of people over another will inevitably fail….

"In Ankara, I made clear that America is not—and never will be—at war with Islam…. Because we reject the same thing that people of all faiths reject: the killing of innocent men, women and children….

"I am aware that some question or justify the events of 9/11….The victims were innocent men, women and children from America…

"Make no mistake: We do not want to keep our troops in Afghanistan. We seek no military bases there. It is agonizing for America to lose our young men and women. It is costly and politically difficult to continue this conflict. We would gladly bring every single one of our troops home if we could be confident that there were not violent extremists in Afghanistan and Pakistan determined to kill as many Americans as they possibly can….

"The Holy Koran teaches that whoever kills an innocent, it is as if he has killed all mankind; and whoever saves a person, it is as if he has saved all mankind....

"Unlike Afghanistan, Iraq was a war of choice that provoked strong differences in my country and around the world.... I also believe that events in Iraq have reminded America of the need to use diplomacy and build international consensus to resolve our problems whenever possible....

"Today, America has a dual responsibility: to help Iraq forge a better future—and to leave Iraq to Iraqis. I have made it clear to the Iraqi people that we pursue no bases, and no claim on their territory or resources. Iraq's sovereignty is its own. And that is why I ordered the removal of our combat brigades by next August... [and will] remove combat troops from Iraqi cities by July, and remove all our troops from Iraq by 2012...

"Nine-eleven was an enormous trauma to our country.... [I]n some cases, it led us to act contrary to our ideals.... I have unequivocally prohibited the use of torture by the United States, and I have ordered the prison at Guantánamo Bay closed by early next year.

"So America will defend itself respectful of the sovereignty of nations and the rule of law....

"The second major source of tension that we need to discuss is the situation between Israelis, Palestinians and the Arab world.

"America's strong bonds with Israel are well known. This bond is unbreakable....

"On the other hand, it is also undeniable that the Palestinian people—Muslims and Christians—have suffered in pursuit of a homeland. For more than 60 years they have endured the pain of dislocation. Many wait in refugee camps in the West Bank, Gaza and neighboring lands for a life of peace and security that they have never been able to lead.... So let there be no doubt: The situation for the Palestinian people is intolerable. America will not turn our backs on the legitimate Palestinian aspiration for dignity, opportunity and a state of their own.

"For decades, there has been a stalemate: two peoples with legitimate aspirations, each with a painful history that makes compromise elusive. It is easy to point fingers—for Palestinians to point to the displacement brought about by Israel's founding, and for Israelis to point to the constant hostility and attacks throughout its history from within its borders as well as beyond. But if we see this conflict only from one side or the other, then we will be blind to the truth: The only resolution is for the aspirations of both sides to be met through two states, where Israelis and Palestinians each live in peace and security....

"For centuries, black people in America suffered the lash of the whip as slaves and the humiliation of segregation. But it was not violence that won full and equal rights.

"Hamas must put an end to violence, recognize past agreements, and recognize Israel's right to exist.

"At the same time, Israelis must acknowledge that just as Israel's right to exist cannot be denied, neither can Palestine's. The United States does not accept the legitimacy of continued Israeli settlements. This construction violates previous agreements and undermines efforts to achieve peace. It is time for these settlements to stop.

"Israel must also live up to its obligation to ensure that Palestinians can live and work and develop their society.... Progress in the daily lives of the Palestinian people must be part of a road to peace, and Israel must take concrete steps to enable such progress....

"The Arab-Israeli conflict should no longer be used to distract the people of Arab nations from other problems....

"The third source of tension is our shared interest in the rights and responsibilities of nations on nuclear weapons....

"In the middle of the Cold War, the United States played a role in the overthrow of a democratically elected Iranian government. Since the Islamic revolution, Iran has played a role in acts of hostage-taking and violence against US troops and civilians.... Rather than remain trapped in the past, I have made it clear to Iran's leaders and people that my country is prepared to move forward. The question now is not what Iran is against, but rather what future it wants to build.

"It will be hard to overcome decades of mistrust, but we will proceed with courage, rectitude and resolve. There will be many issues to discuss between our two countries, and we are willing to move forward without preconditions on the basis of mutual respect....

"I understand those who protest that some countries have weapons that others do not. No single nation should pick and choose which nation holds nuclear weapons. And that is why I strongly reaffirmed America's commitment to seek a world in which no nations hold nuclear weapons. Any nation—including Iran—should have the right to access peaceful nuclear power if it complies with its responsibilities under the nuclear Non-Proliferation Treaty."

In these three first issues raised in his speech we find the basic objective of his trip to the Islamic University of Egypt. One cannot blame the new US president for the situation in the Middle East. It is obvious that he wants to find an exit from the colossal mess created there by his predecessors and by the development of events over the last 100 years.

Not even Obama could imagine when he was working in the black communities of Chicago that the terrible effects of a financial crisis would combine with the factors that made possible his election as president in a strongly racist society.

He takes office at an exceptionally complex time for his country and the world. He is trying to resolve problems that he perhaps considers to be simpler than they really are. Centuries of colonial and capitalist exploitation have created a world where a handful of overdeveloped rich countries coexist with other immensely poor countries that provide raw materials and labor. If you add China and India, two emerging nations, the struggle for natural resources and markets presents an entirely new situation on the planet where human survival itself has yet to be guaranteed.

Obama's African roots, his humble background and his amazing ascent awaken hope in many who like victims of a shipwreck try to hold on to a piece of wood in the middle of the storm.

His statement that "any world order that elevates one nation or group of people over another will inevitably fail" is correct, as he is when he declares, "people of all faiths reject the killing of innocent men, women and children" and when he reaffirms to the world his opposition to the use of torture. Generally speaking, several of these statements are theoretically correct; he clearly perceives the need for all countries, without exception of course, to give up their nuclear weapons. Well-known and influential personalities in the United States see this as a great danger, as technology and science generalize access to radioactive material and ways of using it, even in small amounts.

It is still too early to pass judgment on the extent of Obama's commitment to the ideas he presents, and up to what point he stands firm in sustaining, for example, the proposal to look for a peace agreement built on a fair basis, with guarantees for all states in the Middle East.

The current president's main difficulty lies in the fact that the principles he is advocating contradict the policy the superpower has pursued for almost seven decades, from the end of World War II in August 1945. I put aside for the moment the aggressive and expansionist policy applied to the peoples of Latin America, especially Cuba, when the United States was still far from being the most powerful nation in the world.

Each of the guidelines advocated by Obama in Cairo contradicts the interventions and wars promoted by the United States. The first of these wars was the famous Cold War that he mentions in his speech. Ideological differences with the Soviet Union do not justify the hostility toward that state that contributed more than 25 million lives in the war against Nazism. Obama would not be able to remember at this time the 65th anniversary of the Normandy landing and the liberation of Europe if it were not for the blood of the Soviet troops. Those who freed the survivors of the famous Auschwitz concentration camp were Soviet army soldiers. The world was unaware of what was happening there even though quite a few people in Western official circles knew the facts: how millions of Jewish children, women and old people were atrociously murdered, and millions of Russian children, women and old people lost their lives as a result of the brutal Nazi invasion in their quest for "living space." The West granted concessions to Hitler and finally pushed him to occupy and colonize Slavic lands. During World War II, the Soviets were US allies, not enemies.

The United States dropped and tested the effects of two nuclear bombs over Hiroshima and Nagasaki, two defenseless cities. The Japanese who perished there were mainly children, women and old people.

If one were to analyze the wars promoted, supported or waged by the United States in China, Korea, Vietnam, Laos, Kampuchea, among the millions of people who died, many were children, women and old people.

The colonial wars of France and Portugal after World War II had the support of the United States; the coups and interventions in Central America, Panama, Santo Domingo, Grenada, Chile, Paraguay, Uruguay, Peru and Argentina were all promoted and supported by the United States.

Israel was not a nuclear power. The creation of a state in territory from which the Jews were driven into exile by the Roman Empire 2,000 years ago was supported in good faith by the Soviet Union as well as other countries in the world. On the triumph of the Cuban revolution we had relations with that state for more than a decade until its wars of conquest over the Palestinians and other Arab peoples led us to sever them. Total respect for religion and Jewish religious activities has been maintained without any kind of interference.

The United States never opposed Israeli conquest of Arab territories, nor did it protest the terrorist methods used against the Palestinians. On the contrary, it created a nuclear power there, one of the most advanced in the world, in the heart of Arab and Muslim territory, creating one of the planet's most dangerous places in the Middle East.

The superpower also used Israel to supply nuclear weapons to the apartheid armies in South Africa to be used against Cuban troops that, alongside Angolan and Namibian forces, were defending the Peoples' Republic of Angola. These are fairly recent events that the current US president surely knows about. Thus, we are not unfamiliar with the aggression and the danger the Israeli nuclear potential represents for peace.

After these three initial points of his speech in Cairo, Obama begins philosophizing and lecturing about US foreign policy: "The fourth issue that I will address is democracy," he said.

"So let me be clear: No system of government can or should be imposed by one nation on any other....

"America does not presume to know what is best for everyone, just as we would not presume to pick the outcome of a peaceful election. But I do have an unyielding belief that all people yearn for certain things: the ability to speak your mind and have a say in how you are governed; confidence in the rule of law and the equal administration of justice... Those are not just American ideas; they are human rights, and that is why we will support them everywhere....

"The fifth issue that we must address together is religious freedom.

"Islam has a proud tradition of tolerance.... I saw it firsthand as a child in Indonesia, where devout Christians worshiped freely in an overwhelmingly Muslim country....

"Among some Muslims, there is a disturbing tendency to measure one's own faith by the rejection of another's.... And fault lines must be closed among Muslims as well, as the divisions between Sunni and Shia have led to tragic violence, particularly in Iraq....

"Likewise, it is important for Western countries to avoid impeding Muslim citizens from practicing religion as they see fit—for instance, by dictating what clothes a Muslim woman should wear. We cannot disguise hostility toward any religion behind the pretence of liberalism....

"I reject the view of some in the West that a woman who chooses to cover her hair is somehow less equal, but I do believe that a woman who is denied an education is denied equality. And it is no coincidence that countries where women are well educated are far more likely to be prosperous."

"Meanwhile the struggle for women's equality continues in many aspects of American life, and in countries around the world.

"Our daughters can contribute just as much to society as our sons, and our common prosperity will be advanced by allowing all humanity—men and women—to reach their full potential....

"The Internet and television can bring knowledge and information, but also offensive sexuality and mindless violence. Trade can bring new wealth and opportunities, but also huge disruptions and changing communities.

"[I]invest in online learning for teachers and children around the world; and create a new online network, so a teenager in Kansas can communicate instantly with a teenager in Cairo....

"[W]e have a responsibility to join together on behalf of the world we seek—a world where extremists no longer threaten our people, and American troops have come home; a world where Israelis and Palestinians are each secure in a state of their own, and nuclear energy is used for peaceful purposes… That is the world we seek. But we can only achieve it together.

"It is easier to start wars than to end them…. that we do unto others as we would have them do unto us….

"We have the power to make the world we seek, but only if we have the courage to make a new beginning, keeping in mind what has been written.

"The Holy Koran tells us: 'O mankind! We have created you male and a female; and we have made you into nations and tribes so that you may know one another.'

"The Talmud tells us: 'The whole of the Torah is for the purpose of promoting peace.'

"The Holy Bible tells us: 'Blessed are the peacemakers, for they shall be called sons of God.'

"The people of the world can live together in peace."

As you can see, tackling the fourth issue in his speech at Al-Azhar University Obama stumbles into a contradiction. After beginning his words with a maxim as is his custom, saying, "No system of government can or should be imposed by one nation on any other," a principle included in the United Nations Charter as a fundamental element of international law, he immediately contradicts himself with a declaration of faith that transforms the United States into the supreme judge of democratic values and human rights.

Then he refers to subjects related to economic development and equal opportunities. He makes promises to the Arab world; he points out advantages and contradictions. In reality, this appears to be a public relations campaign carried out by the United States aimed at Muslim countries; in any case, this is better than threatening to destroy them with bombs.

At the end of the speech there is quite a mix of themes.

If one takes into account the length of his speech, without using notes, the number of lapses is negligible as compared with his predecessor who used to make a mistake in every sentence. He is a very good communicator.

I tend to observe historical, political and religious ceremonies with interest.

This one at Al-Azhar University seemed to be unreal. Not even Pope Benedict XVI has spoken such ecumenical phrases as Obama did. For a moment I imagined the pious Muslim, Catholic, Christian or Jew, or someone from any other religion, listening to the president in the spacious hall of Al-Azhar University. At a certain point I couldn't tell whether he was in a Catholic cathedral, a Christian church, a mosque or a synagogue.

He left early for Germany. For three days he toured politically significant sites. He participated and spoke at commemorative ceremonies. He visited museums, received his family and dined at famous restaurants. He has an impressive capacity for work. It will be some time before we see anything like this again.

June 8, 2009

Seven Daggers at the Heart of the Americas

I read and reread the articles written by clever personalities, some better known than others, who are published in various media outlets drawing information from sources nobody questions.

Throughout the world, the people living on this planet face great economic and environmental risks as well as the risk of war due to US policies, but no region of the world is as threatened by such a hegemonic power as that country's neighbors—the peoples of this continent's south.

The presence of such a powerful empire—with its military bases, nuclear submarines and aircraft carriers; modern warships and sophisticated fighter planes that can carry all kinds of weapons, deployed on every continent and ocean; with hundreds of thousands of troops and a government that claims absolute impunity for them—is the most important headache for any government, be it a leftist, rightist or center government, an ally of the United States or not.

The problem for those of us who are its neighbors is not that it is a different country with a different language. There are North Americans of every color and background. They are people just like us with all kinds of feelings, in one sense or another. The drama is the system developed there and imposed on everyone else. That system is not new to the use of force and to the methods of domination that have prevailed throughout history; what is new is the era in which we are living. Approaching the issue from a traditional perspective would be a mistake and no one would benefit. Reading and becoming acquainted with the ideas of the advocates of that system can be very educational for it helps to become aware of the nature of a system built on a continuous appeal to selfishness and to people's most basic instincts.

Without believing in the value of consciousness and its capacity to prevail over instincts, it would be impossible to speak of a hope for change in any period of the very short history of humankind. Nor would it be possible to understand the formidable obstacles confronting the various political leaders of the Latin American and Ibero-American nations in the hemisphere. In any case, until the famous discovery of the Americas, the peoples living in this part of the world over tens of thousands of years had no traits of the Latin, Iberian or European peoples and their features resembled more those of the Asian peoples where their ancestors had come from. Today, we can find them on the faces of the indigenous people in Mexico, Central America, Venezuela, Colombia, Ecuador, Brazil, Peru, Bolivia, Paraguay and Chile, a country where the Araucanians wrote enduring pages of history. In certain areas of Canada and Alaska indigenous roots are preserved as purely as they can be, but in the continental United States a large part of the ancient peoples was exterminated by the white conquerors.

As everybody knows, millions of Africans were uprooted from their lands and brought to work as slaves in this hemisphere. In some countries like Haiti and a large part of the Caribbean Islands their descendants make up the majority of the population, and they are a large sector in some other countries. In the United States, there are tens of millions of people of African descent who, as a rule, are the poorest and most discriminated against.

For centuries that country claimed privileges over our continent. At the time of José Martí, it tried to impose a single currency based on gold, a metal whose value has been the steadiest through history. In general, international trade was based on gold; but that is not the case today. Since the days of Nixon's administration, world trade has developed on the basis of the paper money printed by the United States, the dollar, a currency today worth about 27 times less than in the early 1970s—one of the many ways the rest of the world is dominated and defrauded. At the present moment, however, other currencies are taking the place of the dollar in international trade and hard currency reserves.

Thus, while the value of the empire's currency is decreasing, its military force is increasing and the state-of-the-art technology and science monopolized by the superpower are largely directed to weapons development. At present, this includes not only thousands of nuclear missiles and the modern destructive power of conventional weapons, but also guided planes piloted by robots. This is not just a fantasy. Some of these aircraft are being used in Afghanistan and elsewhere. Recent reports indicate that in the relatively near future, by the year 2020—long before the Antarctic icecap melts—the empire plans to have among its 2,500 war planes, 1,100 fifth-generation F-35 and F-22 fighter-bombers. Just to give an idea of that potential, suffice it to say that the aircraft used at the Soto Cano base in Honduras to train that country's pilots are F-5, and the ones supplied to the Venezuelan air force—prior to Chávez—and to Chile and other countries, were small F-16 squadrons.

Even more significant is the empire's plan for the next 30 years anticipating that every US combat aircraft, from fighter planes to heavy bombers and tanker planes, are to be piloted by robots.

The world does not need such military might; but it is a necessity for the economic system that the empire imposes on the world.

Anyone can understand that if robots can replace combat pilots, they can also replace the workers in many factories. The free-trade agreements that the empire is trying to impose on the countries of this hemisphere mean that these workers will have to compete with the advanced technology and the robots of Yankee industries.

Robots do not go on strike; they are obedient and disciplined. We have seen on TV machinery that can pick apples and other fruits. The question could also be asked of American workers: Where will the jobs be? What future does capitalism with no borders, in its advanced development stage, offer people?

In light of this and other realities, the leaders of UNASUR, MERCOSUR, the Rio Group and others cannot avoid the very good question raised by Venezuela: What is the meaning of the military and naval bases the United States wants to set up around Venezuela and in the heart of South America?

I remember that a few years back, when relations between Colombia and Venezuela, two sister nations bound by geography and history, were dangerously tense Cuba quietly promoted significant steps leading to peace between them. Cuba will never encourage war between sister nations. Historical experience, the "Manifest Destiny" claimed and applied by the United States and the weak accusations that Venezuela has supplied weapons to the FARC [in Colombia], combined with the negotiations aimed at granting to the US armed forces seven sites in that country to be used by their air and naval troops, are leaving Venezuela no other choice but to invest in weaponry the resources that could be used for economic and social programs and cooperation with other countries of the region that have fewer resources and development. Venezuela's military build-up is not aimed against the fraternal people of Colombia but against the empire that has already tried to overthrow the [Bolivarian] revolution and today intends to install sophisticated weapons near the Venezuelan border.

It would be a serious mistake to believe that only Venezuela is being threatened here. In reality, every country in the south of the continent is under threat. Not one of them will be able to avoid the issue as some of them have already stated.

Present and future generations will pass judgment on their leaders for the way they conduct themselves at this moment. It is not only the United States, but the United States and the system. What does it offer? What does it want?

It offers the Free Trade Area of the Americas [FTAA], that is, the early ruin of our countries: free transit of goods and capital, but not free transit of people. They are now afraid that the opulent consumerist society is being inundated by poor Hispanics, indigenous people, blacks, mulattos and whites who cannot find jobs in their own countries. They return everyone who commits an offence or whom they do not need; quite often these people are killed before they enter the United States or are returned like animals when they are not required. Twelve million Latin American and Caribbean immigrants remain in the United States illegally. A new economy has emerged in our countries, especially in the smallest and poorest: remittances. In times of crisis, this strikes mostly the immigrants and their families. Parents and children are separated, sometimes forever. If the immigrant is of military age, he is given the chance to enlist to fight thousands of miles away from home "on behalf of freedom and democracy," and if they are not killed, on their return they are given the right to become US citizens. Then, as they are well trained they are offered the possibility of a contract, not as regular soldiers but as civilian soldiers for the private companies that provide services to the imperial wars of conquest.

There are other extremely serious dangers. There are always news reports of immigrants from Mexico and other countries of our region dying as they try to cross the US-Mexican border. The number of victims each year widely exceeds the total number of those who lost their lives in almost 28 years of the existence of the famous Berlin Wall.

But what is most incredible is that there is hardly any international news about the war that is taking thousands of lives every year. In 2009, more Mexicans have been killed than the number of US soldiers who died during Bush's war on Iraq.

The cause of the war in Mexico is the largest market for drugs in the world: the US market. But there is no war going on in US territory between the police and the military fighting the drug-traffickers.

Instead, the war has been exported to Mexico and Central America, especially to the land of the Aztecs, which is closer to the United States. Dreadful images of dead bodies are shown on TV while reports keep coming in of people murdered in the surgery rooms where their lives were being saved. None of these images originates from US territory.

Such a wave of violence and bloodshed is expanding throughout the countries of South America, affecting them to a greater or lesser extent. Where does the money come from if not from the insatiable US market? Similarly, consumption tends to extend to the rest of the countries in the region resulting in more victims and direct or indirect damage than AIDS, malaria and all other illnesses put together.

The imperial plans for domination are preceded by huge sums of money allocated to the task of deceiving and misinforming the public. For this purpose, they have the full complicity of the oligarchy, the bourgeoisie, the rightist intelligentsia and the media. They are experts in spreading the lies and contradictions of the politicians.

The fate of humankind must not be left in the hands of robots transformed into people or people transformed into robots.

In the year 2010, the US government will promote its policy through the State Department and USAID spending $2.2 billion—12 percent more than the Bush administration allocated in the last year of its second term—and almost $450 million of this will be used to prove that the tyranny imposed on the world represents democracy and respect for human rights.

They constantly appeal to human beings' instincts and selfishness; they despise the value of education and consciousness. The resistance put up by the Cuban people throughout 50 years is clear. Resistance is the weapon that people can never give up. The Puerto Ricans were able to stop the military exercises in Vieques by standing on the site of the firing range.

Bolívar's homeland today is the country they are most worried about because of its historical role in the struggle for the independence of the peoples of the Americas. Cubans working there as health-care and other specialists, educators, physical education and sports teachers, agricultural technicians and specialists in other areas should do their best to fulfill their internationalist duty to prove that the people can put up a resistance and carry forward the most sacred principles of human society. Otherwise, the empire will destroy civilization and even the human race itself.

August 5, 2009

The Empire and the Robots

A while ago I dealt with US plans to impose the absolute superiority of its air force as an instrument of domination on the rest of the world. I mentioned the project that by 2020 they would have more than 1,000 latest generation bombers and F-22 and F-35 fighter planes in their fleet of 2,500 military aircraft. In 20 years, every single one of their war planes will be robot-operated.

Military budgets always count on the support of the immense majority of US legislators. There is hardly any state in the Union where employment does not depend in part on the defense industries.

On a global level, the equivalent value of military expenses has doubled in the last 10 years as if there were no danger at all of any crisis. At this moment, it is the most prosperous industry on the planet.

By 2008, approximately $1.5 trillion invested in defense budgets. The United States spends 42 percent of world expenses in this area—$607 billion—not including war expenses, while the number of people who go hungry in the world has reached the figure of one billion.

Two days ago a Western news dispatch stated that in mid-August the US Army exhibited a tele-guided helicopter along with robots capable of working as sappers, 2,500 of which have been sent into combat zones.

A company marketing robots maintained the new technology would revolutionize the manner of directing the war. It has been published that in 2003 the United States barely had enough robots in its arsenal and, according to AFP, "today it has 10,000 land vehicles as well as 7,000 air devices, from the small Raven that can be hand-launched right up to the gigantic Global Hawk, a spy plane 13 meters long and with a 35-meter wingspan capable of flying at great altitudes for 35 hours." This dispatch lists other weapons as well.

While the United States is spending such huge figures in the technology of killing, the president of that country is sweating buckets trying to bring health services to 50 million Americans who don't have them. There is such confusion that the new president said he felt he was closer than ever to achieving reform of the health-care system but that the battle is becoming fierce.

He added that history is clear: Every time health-care reform seems to be closer on the horizon, special interests fight with everything they've got applying leverage, launching publicity campaigns and using their political allies to frighten the US people.

The fact is that in Los Angeles, 8,000 people—most of them unemployed, according to the press—turned up to a stadium to receive medical care from a traveling free clinic that provides services to the Third World. The crowd had spent the night there. Some of them had traveled from as far away as hundreds of miles.

"What do I care whether it's socialist or not? We're the only country in the world where the most vulnerable people have nothing," said a college-educated woman from a black neighborhood.

According to the report a blood test can cost $500 and routine dental treatment more than $1,000 dollars.

What kind of hope can a society like that offer the world?

The lobbyists in Congress make their profits working against a simple law intended to provide medical care to tens of millions of poor people (mostly blacks and Latinos) who need it. Even a blockaded country like Cuba has been able to do this and is even cooperating with dozens of countries in the Third World.

If robots in the hands of the transnationals can replace imperial soldiers in the wars of conquest, who will stop the transnationals in their quest for a market for their commodities? Just as they have flooded the world with automobiles that today compete with humankind for the consumption of nonrenewable energy and are even converting food into fuel, so too can they flood the world with robots that would displace millions of workers from their workplaces.

Better still, scientists could also design robots capable of governing; that way they could spare the US government and Congress that terrible, contradictory and confusing work.

No doubt they would do it better and cheaper.

August 19, 2009

I Wish I Were Wrong!

I was amazed to read the wire services issued during the weekend about US domestic policy, showing a systematic decline in President Barack Obama's popularity. His surprising electoral victory would not have been possible without the deep political and economic crisis affecting his country. The [number of] US soldiers killed or wounded in Iraq, the scandal about torture and secret prisons, and the loss of jobs and housing had all shaken US society. The economic crisis was spreading throughout the planet, thus increasing poverty and hunger in Third World countries.

Such circumstances made it possible for Obama to run for office and be elected in a traditionally racist society. No less than 90 percent of the poor and discriminated against black people, most of the Latino voters and a broad working and middle class white minority, especially the youth, voted for him.

It was only logical for those North Americans supporting him to entertain a great deal of hope. After eight years of adventurism, demagogy and lies, which led to the death of thousands of US soldiers and almost one million Iraqis in a war of conquest over that Muslim country's oil, a country that had nothing whatsoever to do with the atrocious attack on the Twin Towers, the US people felt tired and ashamed.

Moreover, quite a few people in Africa and elsewhere got excited about the idea that US foreign policy would change.

However, an elementary reality check would have been enough to moderate expectations of a possible political change in the United States after the election of the new president.

Certainly, Obama had opposed the war launched by Bush against Iraq long before many others in the US Congress did so. Since his youth, he knew the humiliations of racial discrimination, and like many other Americans, he admired Martin Luther King, Jr., the outstanding fighter for civil rights.

Obama was born, educated, went into politics and managed to be successful within the US imperial capitalist system. He neither wished nor could he change the system. Curiously enough, despite this, the extreme right hates him for being an African American and opposes anything the president does to improve that country's tarnished image.

He has come to understand that the United States, with hardly 4 percent of the world's population, consumes about 25 percent of its fossil fuels, and is the biggest source of emissions of pollutant gases on the planet.

Bush, in his ravings, never even signed the Kyoto Protocol.

Obama, for his part, intends to implement stricter rules against tax evasion. For example, reportedly, the Swiss banks will supply data about approximately 4,500 financial accounts of a total of 52,000 accounts owned by US citizens suspected of tax evasion.

A few weeks ago in Europe, Obama committed himself before the G-8 countries, especially France and Germany, to put an end to the use of fiscal havens by his country in order to inject huge amounts of US dollars into the world economy.

He offered health care to almost 50 million citizens who had no medical insurance.

He promised the US people that he would grease the wheels of industrial production, halt rising unemployment and resume growth.

He promised the 12 million Hispanic illegal immigrants he would end the cruel raids and the inhumane treatment they receive.

He made other promises that I will not list, but none of them questions the system of imperial capitalist domination.

The powerful extreme right will not tolerate any single measure that might mean even a minimal reduction of its prerogatives.

I will just limit myself to refer to some reports published in recent days by US press agencies.

August 21:

According to a poll published by the *Washington Post*, the confidence of US citizens in President Barack Obama's leadership has substantially decreased.

In the midst of increasing opposition to health-care reform, the telephone poll conducted by that newspaper and the ABC TV network among 1,001 adults from August 13 to 17 revealed that 49 percent of respondents believe that Obama would be able to significantly improve the US health-care system. This result is a 20 percent decrease compared to the period before Obama came to office.

Fifty five percent of the respondents believe that the general situation in the United States is not going well, compared to 48 percent in April.

The fierce debate over the health-care reform in the United States is evidence of an extremism that is a source of concern among experts; they are alarmed about the presence of armed men in popular gatherings, the drawing of swastikas and the images of Hitler.

Experts in hate crimes have recommended the close monitoring of these extremists. While many Democrats have felt overwhelmed by the protests, others have decided to confront their fellow compatriots directly.

The young woman who carried a manipulated picture of Obama, wearing a Hitler-style moustache, believed the president would create "death panels" that would support the euthanasia of senior citizens with terminal illnesses.

According to reports, there are those who pretend to be deaf and resort to conveying messages of hatred and extremism, which Brad Garrett, a former agent of the Federal Bureau of Investigation (FBI), deems as alarming.

Last week Garrett told the ABC network that we were certainly living through scary times, and added that the secret services are afraid that something may happen to Obama.

According to reports, just last Monday, about 12 people proudly showed off their weapons outside the Phoenix Convention Center in Arizona, where the president was delivering a speech to war veterans in which, among other things, he defended his health-care reform.

It was reported that another man carried a gun bearing the inscription: "The time has come to refresh the tree of liberty," which invoked the words of President Thomas Jefferson (1801-1809) when he said "the tree of liberty must be refreshed … by the blood of patriots and tyrants."

Some messages were even more explicit, wishing for the death of Obama, Michelle and their two daughters.

These incidents show that hatred has penetrated America's politics more strongly than ever before.

Larry Berman, from the University of California, who has written 12 books about the US presidency, told the EFE news agency that right now we are talking about people who shout and carry pictures of Obama as a Nazi and refer to the term "socialist" with contempt. He believes this is partly explained by the persistent legacy of racism.

After the *New York Times* reported [on August 20] that the CIA had hired Blackwater back in 2004 to perform the tasks of planning, training and surveillance, the newspaper revealed further details [on August 21] about the activities entrusted to that controversial private security company whose current name is "Xe."

The newspaper revealed that the Central Intelligence Agency recruited several Blackwater agents to install bombs on board drones in order to kill Al Qaeda leaders.

According to information revealed by government officials to the *New York Times*, these operations were carried out in bases located in Pakistan and Afghanistan, where the private company equipped the planes with Hellfire missiles and laser-guided bombs.

It was reported that the current CIA director, Leon Panetta, decided at some point in time to cancel the program and explain to Congress in June the nature of the collaboration between Blackwater and the CIA.

According to the news report, Blackwater's collaboration ended a few years before Panetta was appointed as CIA chief, because agency officials themselves questioned the convenience of having external agents participating in programs of selective assassinations.

Blackwater is said to have been the main private security company in charge of protecting US staff in Iraq during the George W. Bush administration.

Apparently, its aggressive tactics were criticized on different occasions. The most serious case occurred in September 2007, when some agents from the company killed 17 Iraqi civilians.

After considering the record figures of suicides and the wave of depression spreading among its soldiers, the US Army is said to be, little by little, creating some special groups whose task will be to enhance its troops' resistance against war-related emotional stress.

August 22:

On this day US President Barack Obama is said to have harshly criticized those who oppose his plan to reform the health-care system in his country, and accused them of disseminating false and distorted information.

According to reports, as he himself has pointed out in his speeches, the objective of the reform is to end rapidly increasing costs and ensure health coverage for almost 50 million Americans who have no health insurance.

According to the news reports, this should have been an honest debate, not dominated by the deliberately false and distorted reports that have been disseminated by those who would benefit the most if things continue the way they are.

According to the *New York Times* today, the US State Department has continued funding Blackwater (now called Xe Services), the private company of mercenaries who were involved in the assassination of Al Qaeda leaders.

It was reported that the governor of the state of New York, David Paterson, stated last Friday that the media had resorted to the use of racial stereotypes in its coverage of black officials like him, President Obama and the governor of Massachusetts, Deval Patrick.

It is said that the White House has estimated that the budget deficit during the next decade will amount to $2 trillion more than the recent estimate, which would be a storming blow for President Barack Obama and his plans to create a public health system largely financed by the state.

Ten-year forecasts are said to be very volatile and could vary with time. However, the new deficit estimate will reportedly pose serious problems for Obama in Congress, and will cause a huge anxiety among the foreigners who are financing America's public debt, especially China. Almost all economists consider them to be unsustainable even if there were a mass devaluation of the US dollar.

August 23:

The top ranking military who commands the US Army is said to have expressed his concern last Sunday about the loss of popular support in his country for the war in Afghanistan, while indicating that the country continued to be vulnerable to the attacks of the extremists.

Mike Mullen, the chief of the military joint command said the situation in Afghanistan was serious and deteriorating, and added that in the last two years, the Taliban insurrection has improved and become more specialized.

In an interview aired by the NBC TV network, Mullen did not specify whether or not it would be necessary to send more troops.

According to reports, a little over 50 percent of the respondents in the poll conducted by the *Washington Post* and the ABC TV network, the results of which were published recently, said the war in Afghanistan was not worthwhile.

Reportedly, by the end of 2009, the United States will have three times more soldiers than the 20,000 who were deployed in Afghanistan three years ago.

Confusion is rampant in US society.

September 11, [2009] will mark the eighth year since the fateful 9/11. On that same day, at Havana's sports stadium, we warned that war was not the way to end terrorism.

The strategy of withdrawing troops from Iraq and sending them to the Afghan war to fight the Taliban is wrong. The Soviet Union was trapped in a quagmire there. The European allies of the United States will be ever more reluctant to see the blood of their soldiers shed in that country.

Mullen's concern over the popularity of that war is not far off the mark. Those who perpetrated the attack on September 11, 2001, against the Twin Towers were trained by the United States.

The Taliban is an Afghan nationalist movement that had nothing to do with that event. Al Qaeda, an organization that has been financed by the CIA since 1979 and was used against the Soviet Union during the Cold War, was the organization that masterminded that attack 22 years later.

There are still some shadowy events that need further clarification for the benefit of international public opinion.

Obama has inherited these problems from Bush.

I do not have the slightest doubt that the racist right will do its best to try to wear him out by hindering his program and leaving him out the game, one way or the other, at the lowest possible political cost.

I wish I were wrong!

August 24, 2009

The Serious Obama

Bolivarian President Hugo Chávez made a really clever remark when he referred to the "enigma of the two Obamas."

The serious Obama spoke today. Recently, I acknowledged two positive actions: his attempt to make health care available to the 47 million Americans who don't have access to it, and his concern about climate change.

What I said yesterday about the imminent threat to the human species might sound pessimistic but it is not far from reality. The views of many heads of state on the ignored and neglected issue of climate change are still unknown.

As the representative of the country hosting the United Nations high-level meeting on the issue, Obama was the first to express his opinion. What did he say? I will refer to the substance of his remarks:

> He recognizes that the threat to the planet is serious and growing.
>
> History will pass judgment on the response to this environmental challenge.
>
> There is no nation, big or small, that can avoid the impact of climate change.
>
> There is a daily increase of the high tides lashing against the coastlines while more intensive storms and floods are threatening our continents.
>
> The security and stability of every nation are in danger.
>
> Climate has been placed at the top of the international agenda, from China to Brazil, from India to Mexico, Africa and Europe.
>
> There can be significant steps if we are all united.

We understand the seriousness of the situation and are determined to act on it.

We were not there to celebrate any progress.

Much remains to be done.

It will not be an easy job.

The most difficult part of the road is ahead of us.

This is happening at a time when to many the priority is to revitalize their economies.

We all have doubts about the climate challenge. Difficulties and doubts are no excuse not to act.

Each of us should do their share so that our economies can grow without endangering the planet.

We should turn Copenhagen into a significant step forward in the climate debate.

We should not allow for old divisions to jeopardize the united quest for solutions.

The developed nations have caused most of the damage and should thus take responsibility for it.

We will not overcome this challenge unless we are united.

We know these nations, particularly the most vulnerable, do not have the same resources to combat climate change.

The future is not a choice between economic growth and a clean planet because survival depends on both.

It is our responsibility to provide technical and financial assistance to these nations.

We are seeking an agreement that would enhance the quality of life of the peoples without disturbing the planet.

We know the future depends on a global commitment.

But it is a long and tough road and we have no time to make the journey.

The problem now is that everything he has said contradicts what the United States has been doing for over 150 years, especially from the moment—at the end of World War II—when it imposed the Bretton Woods accord and became the master of the world economy.

The hundreds of US military bases set up in scores of countries on every continent; their aircraft carriers and naval fleets; their thousands of nuclear weapons; their wars of conquest; their military-industrial complex and their arms trade are incompatible with the survival of our species. Likewise, consumer societies are incompatible with the idea of economic growth and a clean planet. The unlimited waste of nonrenewable natural resources—especially oil and gas accumulated throughout hundreds of millions of years and depleted in barely two centuries at the current rate of consumption—has been the major cause of climate change. Even if the emissions of the industrialized nations were reduced, which would be commendable, it is a reality that 5.2 billion people on planet Earth—that is, three-quarters of the world's population—live in countries that are still in various stages of development and will therefore demand an enormous input of coal, oil, natural gas and other nonrenewable resources that, according to the consumption patterns established by the capitalist economies, are incompatible with the objective of saving the human species.

It would not be fair to blame the serious Obama for this enigma of what has occurred up to the present time, but nor would it be fair to have the other Obama make us believe that humanity can be preserved under the prevailing rules of the world economy.

The president of the United States has conceded that the developed nations have caused most of the damage and should take responsibility for it. This was certainly a brave gesture.

It would also be fair to concede that no other president of the United States would have had the courage to say what he has said.

September 22, 2009

A Nobel Prize for Evo

If Obama was awarded the Nobel Peace Prize for winning the elections in a racist society, despite his being an African American, Evo [Morales] deserves it for winning the presidential election in Bolivia, despite his being indigenous and having delivered on his promises. For the first time in both countries, a member of their respective ethnic groups has won the presidency.

I have said several times that Obama is a clever and cultivated man in a social and political system he believes in. He wishes to bring health care to nearly 50 million Americans, to rescue the economy from its profound crisis and to improve the image of the United States, which has deteriorated as a result of genocidal wars and torture. He neither plans nor wishes to change his country's political and economic system; nor could he do it.

The Nobel Peace Prize has been awarded to three American presidents, one former president and one candidate to the presidency. The first was Theodore Roosevelt elected in 1901. He was one of the Rough Riders who landed in Cuba with riders but no horses in the wake of the US intervention in 1898 aimed at preventing the independence of our homeland.

The second was Thomas Woodrow Wilson who dragged the United States to the first world war for the distribution of the world's resources. The extremely severe conditions he imposed on a vanquished Germany, through the Versailles Treaty, set the foundations for the emergence of fascism and the outbreak of World War II.

The third has been Barack Obama.

Carter was the ex-president who received the Nobel Prize a few years after leaving office. He was certainly one of the few presidents of that country who would not order the murder of an adversary, as others did. He returned the Panama Canal, opened the US Interests Section in Havana and prevented large budget deficits as well as the squandering of money to benefit the military-industrial complex as Reagan had done.

The candidate was Al Gore—when he was already vice-president. He was the best-informed US politician on the dreadful consequences of climate change. As a presidential candidate, he was the victim of an electoral fraud and stripped of victory by George W. Bush.

Views have been deeply divided concerning the recipient of this award. Many people question the ethics or perceive obvious contradictions in the surprise decision. They would have rather seen the prize given for an accomplished task. The Nobel Peace Prize has not always been presented to people deserving that distinction. On occasion it has been criticized by resentful and arrogant people, or even worse. On hearing the news, Lech Walesa scornfully remarked: "Who, Obama? It's too soon. He has not had time to do anything."

In our Cuban press and in *CubaDebate*, honest revolutionary compañeros have expressed their criticisms. One wrote: "The same week in which Obama was granted the Nobel Peace Prize, the US Senate passed the largest military budget in its history: $626 billion." Another journalist commented on the TV news: "What has Obama done to deserve that award?" And still another asked: "And what about the Afghan war and the increased number of bombings?" These views are based on reality.

In Rome, filmmaker Michael Moore made a scathing comment: "Congratulations, President Obama, for the Nobel Peace Prize; now, please, earn it."

I am sure that Obama agrees with Moore's remark. He is clever enough to understand the circumstances of this case. He knows he has not earned the award yet. That morning he said he was under the impression that he did not deserve to be in the company of so many inspiring personalities who have been honored with that prize.

The celebrated committee that assigns the Nobel Peace Prize is made up of five people who are all members of the Swedish parliament. A spokesman said it was a unanimous vote. One wonders whether or not the prizewinner was consulted and if such a decision can be made without giving that person advance notice.

The moral judgment would be different depending on whether or not he had prior knowledge of the prize's allocation. The same could be said of those who decided to present it to him.

Perhaps it would be worthwhile creating the Nobel Transparency Prize.

However, nobody has brought up Evo's name.

It is obvious that for the first time in Bolivian history a man who is every inch an indigenous Aymara has become president of that state founded by "The Liberator," Simón Bolívar, after the battle at Ayacucho, when the last Spanish viceroy surrendered to General Antonio José de Sucre.

At the time Bolivia's territory was 1,464,855 square miles. Its population was basically made up by descendants of the Aymara-Quechua civilization whose knowledge in various fields elicits the admiration of the world. They had rebelled against their oppressors more than once.

Despite the common blood and culture binding them, the fratricidal and pro-imperialist oligarchs of the neighboring states snatched 779,552 square miles from Bolivia, that is, more than half its territory. It is a known fact that over centuries, gold, silver and other resources were extracted from Bolivia by the privileged owners of the country's economy. Huge copper deposits, the largest in the world, as well as other minerals had been stolen from them after independence through one of the wars promoted by the British and Yankee imperialists.

Despite all this, Bolivia is a country with large oil and gas deposits as well as the largest known reserves of lithium, a mineral currently in great demand for the storage and use of energy.

Before his sixth birthday, Evo Morales, a very poor indigenous peasant, walked through the Andes with his father tending the llamas of his community. He had to herd the animals for two weeks to the market where they were sold to pay for food for the community. In response to a question I asked him about this experience, Evo told me he "took shelter in the one-thousand star hotel," a beautiful way of describing the clear skies on the mountains where telescopes are sometimes placed.

In those difficult days of his childhood, the only alternative for the peasants in his community was to cut sugarcane in the Argentine province of Jujuy, where part of the Aymara community went to work during the harvesting season.

Not far from La Higuera, where after being wounded and disarmed Che [Guevara] was murdered on October 9, 1967, Evo—who had been born on the 26th of that same month in 1959—was not yet eight years old. He learned to read and write in Spanish in a small public school, a 3.2-mile walk from the one-room shack he shared with his parents and siblings.

During his precarious childhood, Evo would go wherever there was a teacher. It was from his race that he learned three ethical principles: don't lie, don't steal and don't be weak.

At the age of 13, his father allowed him to move to San Pedro de Oruro to attend senior high school. One of his biographers has related that he did better in geography, history and philosophy than in physics and mathematics. The most important thing is that, in order to pay for school, Evo woke at 2:00 in the morning to work as a baker, a construction worker and any other laboring job he could find. He attended school in the afternoon. His classmates admired him and helped him. From early childhood he learned how to play wind instruments and was even a trumpet player in a prestigious band in Oruro.

As a teenager he organized and was the captain of his community's soccer team. But, access to the university was beyond the reach of a poor Aymara child.

After completing senior high school, he did military service and then returned to his community on the mountain tops. Later, poverty and natural disasters forced the family to migrate to the subtropical area known as El Chapare, where they managed to have a plot of land. His father passed away in 1983, when Evo was 23 years old. He worked hard on the land but he was a born fighter; he organized the workers and created trade unions thus filling a space neglected by the government.

The conditions for a social revolution in Bolivia had been maturing over the past 50 years. The revolution broke out in that country with Victor Paz Estenssoro's Revolutionary Nationalist Movement (MNR) on April 9, 1952, that is, before the start of our armed struggle [in Cuba]. The revolutionary miners defeated the repressive forces and the MNR seized power.

The revolutionary objectives in Bolivia were not attained and in 1956, according to some well-informed people, the process began to decline. On January 1, 1959, the revolution triumphed in Cuba, and three years later, in January 1962, our homeland was expelled from the Organization of American States. Bolivia abstained from this vote. Later, every government except Mexico severed relations with Cuba.

The divisions in the international revolutionary movement had an impact on Bolivia. Time passed with over 40 years of blockade on Cuba; neoliberalism had devastating consequences; then came the Bolivarian revolution in Venezuela and the ALBA and, most importantly, Evo and his MAS [party] in Bolivia.

It would be hard to summarize Evo's rich history in a few pages. I will only say that Evo has prevailed over wicked and slanderous imperialist campaigns, coups and interference in the internal affairs of his country and he has defended Bolivia's sovereignty and the right of its thousand-year-old people to have their traditions respected. "Coca is not cocaine," he retorted to the largest marijuana producer and drug consumer in the world, whose market has sustained organized crime that costs thousands of lives in Mexico every year. Two of the countries where the Yankee troops and their military bases are stationed are the largest drug producers on the planet.

The deadly trap of drug trafficking has failed to catch Bolivia, Venezuela and Ecuador, revolutionary countries members of ALBA which, like Cuba, are aware of what they can and should do to bring health care, education and well-being to their peoples. They do not need foreign troops to combat drug trafficking.

Bolivia is fostering a wonderful project under the leadership of an Aymara president with the support of his people. Illiteracy was eradicated in less than three years: 824,101 Bolivians learned to read and write; 24,699 did so also in Aymara and 13,599 in Quechua. Bolivia is the third country [in Latin America] to be free of illiteracy, following Cuba and Venezuela.

It provides free health care to millions of people who had never had it before. It is one of the seven countries in the world with the largest reduction of infant mortality rate in the last five years and with a real possibility to meet the Millennium Goals before the year 2015, with a similar accomplishment regarding maternal deaths. It has conducted eye surgery on 454,161 people, 75,974 of them Brazilians, Argentines, Peruvians and Paraguayans.

Bolivia has set itself an ambitious social program: every child attending school from first to eighth grade receives an annual grant to pay for school materials. This benefits nearly two million students.

More than 700,000 people over 60 years of age are receiving an annual benefit of about $342.

Every pregnant woman and child under two years of age receives an additional benefit of approximately $257.

Bolivia, one of the three poorest nations in the hemisphere, has brought under state control the country's most important energy and mineral resources, while respecting and compensating every single affected interest. It is advancing carefully because it does not want to take a step backward. Its hard currency reserves have been growing, and now they are no less than three times higher than they were at the beginning of Evo's mandate. It is one of the countries making better use of external cooperation and it is a strong advocate for the environment.

In a very short time, Bolivia has been able to establish the Biometric Electoral Register and approximately 4.7 million voters have registered, that is, nearly a million more than in the last electoral roll that in January 2009 included 3.8 million people.

There will be elections on December 6, [2009]. The people's support for their president will certainly increase. Nothing has stopped his growing prestige and popularity.

Why is he not awarded the Nobel Peace Prize? I understand he has a great disadvantage: He is not the president of the United States of America.

October 15, 2009

The Annexation of Colombia to the United States

Anyone who is reasonably well informed can see immediately that the sweetened Supplemental Agreement for Cooperation and Technical Assistance in Defense and Security between the governments of Colombia and the United States signed on October 30, and made public on November 2, amounts to the annexation of Colombia to the United States.

The agreement presents theoreticians and politicians with a conundrum. It wouldn't be honest to keep silent now and speak later about sovereignty, democracy, human rights, freedom of expression and other delights when a country is being devoured by the empire as easily as a lizard catches flies. The Colombian people are a self-sacrificing, industrious and combative people. I searched the hefty document for a palatable justification but I found none whatsoever.

Of the 48 pages, with 21 lines each, five are used to philosophize on the background of the shameful absorption that turns Colombia into an overseas territory. It is all based on the agreements signed with the United States after the murder of the distinguished progressive leader Jorge Eliécer Gaitán on April 9, 1948, and the establishment on April 30, 1948, of the Organization of American States, discussed by the foreign ministers of the hemisphere at their meeting in Bogotá, with the United States as the boss. During these dramatic days the Colombian oligarchy cut short the life of that [important] leader, thus paving the way for the onset of the armed struggle in Colombia.

The Agreement on Military Assistance between the Republic of Colombia and the United States of April 1952; the agreement related to army, naval and air missions by US forces, signed on October 7, 1974; the 1988 UN Convention against the Illicit Traffic in Narcotic Drugs and Psychotropic Substances; the 2000 UN Convention against Organized Transnational Organized Crime; the 2001 UN Security Council Resolution 1373 and the Inter-American Democratic Charter; the Democratic Security and Defense Policy resolution and others referred to in the abovementioned document, none of them can justify turning a country of 713,592.5 square miles (located in the heart of South America) into a US military base. Colombia's territory is 1.6 times that of Texas, the second largest state of the Union seized from Mexico and later used as a base to conquer with great violence more than half of that country.

On the other hand, over 59 years have passed since Colombian soldiers were sent to faraway Asia, in October 1950, to fight alongside Yankee troops against Chinese and Korean combatants. Now the empire intends to send them to fight against their brothers in Venezuela, Ecuador and other Bolivarian and ALBA countries to crush the Venezuelan revolution as they tried to do with the Cuban revolution in April 1961.

For more than a year and a half before the invasion of Cuba, the Yankee administration fostered, armed and used counterrevolutionary bandits in the Escambray in the same way it is now using the Colombian paramilitary forces against Venezuela.

At the time of the Bay of Pigs attack, the Yankee B-26 aircrafts piloted by mercenaries operated from Nicaragua. Their fighter planes were brought to the theater of operations in an aircraft carrier and the invaders of Cuban origin who landed in our territory were escorted by US warships and by the US Marines. This time their war equipment and troops will be in Colombia posing a threat not only to Venezuela but to every country in Central and South America.

It is really cynical to claim that this infamous agreement is necessary to fight drug trafficking and international terrorism. Cuba has shown that there is no need for foreign troops to prevent the cultivation and trafficking of drugs and to preserve domestic order, even though the United States—the mightiest power on earth—has promoted, financed and armed the terrorists who for decades have attacked the Cuban revolution.

The preservation of domestic peace is a basic prerogative of every government and the presence of Yankee troops in any Latin American country to act on their behalf constitutes blatant foreign interference in their internal affairs that will inevitably be rejected by the people.

A simple reading of the document shows that not only will the Colombian airbases be in the Yankees' hands but also the civilian airports and ultimately any facility that may be useful to the US armed forces. The radio space is also available to that country with a different culture and other interests that have nothing in common with those of the Colombian people.

The US armed forces will have exceptional prerogatives. The occupiers can commit any crime anywhere in Colombia against Colombian families, property and laws and still be unaccountable to that country's authorities. Actually, they have taken diseases and scandalous behavior to many places like the Palmerola military base in Honduras. In Cuba, when they came to visit the neocolony, they sat astride the neck of José Martí's statue in Havana's Central Park. The limit set on the total number of soldiers can be modified on request by the United States, with no restrictions whatsoever. The aircraft carriers and warships visiting the naval bases handed over to them can take as large a crew as they choose, and this can be thousands in only one of their large aircraft carriers.

The agreement, which will remain in force for successive 10-year periods, can't be modified until the end of every period, with a requirement for one year's prior notice. What will the United States do if an administration like that of Johnson, Nixon, Reagan, Bush,

Sr. or Bush, Jr., and others like them is asked to leave Colombia? The Yankees have ousted scores of governments in our hemisphere. How long would a government last in Colombia if it announced such an intention?

Now the politicians in Latin America are faced with a sensitive issue: the fundamental duty of explaining their point of view on the annexation document. I am aware that what is happening in Honduras at this decisive moment is attracting the attention of the media and the foreign ministers of this hemisphere, but the Latin American governments cannot ignore the extremely serious and transcendental events taking place in Colombia.

I have no doubt about the reaction of the peoples [of the continent]; they will feel the dagger being shoved deep inside them, especially in Colombia. They will oppose it! They will never cave in to such ignominy!

Today, the world is facing serious and pressing problems. The whole of humanity is threatened by climate change. European leaders are almost begging on their knees for some kind of agreement in Copenhagen that will prevent the catastrophe. They practically concede that the summit will fail to meet the objective of reaching an agreement that can drastically reduce greenhouse gas emissions and promise to continue struggling to attain it before 2012; however, there is a real risk that an agreement might not be reached until it is too late.

The Third World countries are rightly claiming from the richest and most developed nations hundreds of billion dollars a year to pay for the climate battle.

Does it make sense for the US government to invest time and money in building military bases in Colombia in order to impose on our peoples their hateful tyranny? Along that path, if a disaster is already threatening the world, a greater and more imminent disaster is threatening the empire and it will all be the consequence of the system that exploits and plunders the planet.

November 6, 2009

A Science Fiction Story

I very much regret having to criticize Obama knowing that in his country there are other would-be presidents much worse than he. I am aware that holding that post in the United States today is a major headache. The best example of this is the report in yesterday's edition of *Granma* that said 237 members of the US Congress, or 44 percent, are millionaires. This does not mean that every one of them is an incorrigible reactionary but it is extremely difficult for them to feel like the many millions of Americans who do not have access to medical care, who are unemployed or who need to work very hard to earn their living.

Of course, Obama himself is no beggar; he has millions of dollars. He was a successful professional and his command of language, his eloquence and intellect are unquestionable. Also, he was elected president despite his being an African American, a first in the history of his racist country, which is enduring a profound international economic crisis of its own making.

This is not being "anti-American" as the system and its massive media tend to label their adversaries.

The US people are not to blame; rather they are the victims of a system that is not only unsustainable but—worse still—is incompatible with human life.

The clever and rebellious Obama, who suffered humiliation and racism in his childhood and youth, understands this, but the Obama educated by the system and committed to it and to the methods that took him to the US presidency cannot resist the temptation to pressure, to threaten and even to deceive others.

He is a workaholic. Perhaps no other US president would dare to undertake such an intensive program as he has planned for the next eight days.

According to this plan, he will make an extensive tour of Alaska where he intends to address the troops stationed there. He will be visiting Japan, Singapore, the People's Republic of China and South Korea. He will attend the Asia-Pacific Economic Cooperation forum (APEC) and the meeting of the Association of South East Asian Nations (ASEAN). He will hold talks with the prime minister of Japan and His Majesty Emperor Akihito in the land of the Rising Sun as well as with the prime ministers of Singapore and South Korea and the presidents of Indonesia (Susilo Bambang), Russia (Dmitri Medvedev) and of the People's Republic of China (Hu Jintao). He will be making speeches and giving press conferences. He will be carrying with him his nuclear briefcase, which we hope he will have no need to use during his rushed tour.

His security advisor has said Obama will discuss with the president of Russia the continuance of the START-1 Treaty, set to expire on December 5, 2009. There is no doubt that some reductions in the enormous nuclear arsenal will be agreed upon, even though this will be of no consequence to world peace and the economy.

What is our distinguished friend planning to discuss during his intensive trip? The White House has made a solemn announcement: climate change and economic recovery; nuclear disarmament and the Afghan war; and the risks of war in Iran and in the People's Democratic Republic of Korea. There is plenty of material here to produce a work of fiction.

But how can Obama unravel the problems of climate change when the position of his representatives during the preparatory meetings in Bangkok and Barcelona for the Copenhagen summit on the effects of greenhouse gas emissions was the worst among the industrialized and rich nations. The United States chose not to sign the Kyoto Protocol and the oligarchy of that country is not willing to genuinely cooperate.

How can he contribute to the solution of the grave economic problems afflicting a large part of humanity when, at the end of 2008, the total debt of the United States—including that of federal, state and local administrations, businesses and families—amounted to $57 trillion, that is, over 400 percent of GDP, and the US budget deficit reached almost 13 percent of GDP in the fiscal year 2009, facts Obama is certainly aware of.

What can he offer Hu Jintao when his openly protectionist policies have been aimed against Chinese exports and he is demanding at all costs that the Chinese government revaluates the yuan, an action that would adversely impact on the growing Third World imports from China?

The Brazilian theologian Leonardo Boff, who is no disciple of Karl Marx but an honest Catholic among others who are not willing to cooperate with imperialism in Latin America, said recently, "we are risking our destruction and the devastation of the diversity of life."

He continued: "Almost half of humanity today is living below the poverty line. The wealthiest 20 percent are consuming 82.49 percent of all of the riches on earth while the poorest 20 percent are living on a tiny 1.6 percent." He also quotes the FAO, warning, "in coming years, there will be from 150 to 200 million climate refugees." And then he adds that "humanity is consuming today 30 percent above the regenerating capacity… the planet is giving unmistakable signs that it can take no more."

What he says is true, but Obama and the US Congress have yet to absorb this.

What is he leaving us in the hemisphere? The shameful problem in Honduras and the annexation of Colombia where the United States will set up seven military bases. They also established a military base in Cuba more than 100 years ago that remains there by force. It was in that base [Guantánamo] where they installed the horrible torture center widely known around the world; the same center that Obama has yet to close.

I hold the view that before Obama completes his term there will be between six and eight right-wing governments in Latin America that will be allies of the empire. Furthermore, the US extreme right will try to limit his administration to one term so that there will be a Nixon, a Bush or the likes of a Cheney back in the White House. Then, the significance will be clear of those totally unjustifiable bases today threatening the South American peoples under the pretext of fighting drug trafficking, a problem created by the tens of billions of dollars that organized crime and the producers of drugs in Latin America receive from the United States.

Cuba has shown it only takes justice and social development to fight drugs. In our country, the crime rate per 100,000 people is one of the lowest in the world. No other country in the hemisphere exhibits such a low rate of violence. It is also recognized that, despite the blockade, no other country can boast our high level of education.

The Latin American peoples will resist the onslaught of the empire!

Obama's trip seems like a science fiction story.

November 11, 2009

Obama's Cynical Action was Uncalled For

In the final paragraphs of a "Reflection" entitled "The Bells are Tolling for the Dollar," published two months ago on October 9, I mentioned the climate change problem facing humanity brought on by imperialist capitalism.

With regards to carbon emissions I said: "The United States is not making any real effort but accepting just a 4 percent reduction with respect to the year 1990." At that time, scientists were demanding a minimum of 25 to 40 percent by the year 2020.

Then I added: "In the morning of this Friday 9, the world woke up to the news that 'the good Obama' of the enigma—as explained by Bolivarian President Hugo Chávez Frias at the United Nations—had been awarded the Nobel Peace Prize. I do not always agree with the positions of that institution but I must admit that, at this moment it was, in my view, a positive act. It compensates for the setback Obama experienced in Copenhagen when Rio de Janeiro, and not Chicago, was chosen as the venue for the 2016 Olympic Games, a choice that sparked heated attacks from his right-wing adversaries.

"Many will feel that he has yet to earn the right to receive such an award," I said. "Rather than rewarding the president of the United States, we choose to see that decision as a criticism of the genocidal policy pursued by more than a few presidents of that country who took [the United States] to the crossroads where it is today. That is, [we see it] as a call for peace and for the pursuit of solutions conducive to the survival of the species."

Obviously, I was carefully watching the black president, elected in a racist country afflicted by a deep economic crisis; however, I avoided making a prejudiced judgment based on his campaign statements and his position as leader of the Yankee executive.

Nearly one month later, in another "Reflection" entitled "A Science Fiction Story," I wrote: "The US people are not to blame but rather they are the victims of a system that is not only unsustainable but—worse still—is incompatible with human life.

"The clever and rebellious Obama, who suffered humiliation and racism in his childhood and youth, understands this, but the Obama educated by the system and committed to it and to the methods that took him to the US presidency cannot resist the temptation to pressure, to threaten and even to deceive others.

"He is a workaholic," I continued. "Perhaps no other US president would dare to undertake such an intensive program as he has planned for the next eight days."

In that "Reflection," I analyzed the complexity and contradictions of his long journey through South East Asia and I wondered: "What is our distinguished friend planning to discuss during his intensive journey?" His advisors claimed he would be discussing every issue with China, Russia, Japan, South Korea, and so on, and so forth.

It is clear now that Obama was paving the way for his remarks of December 1, 2009, at West Point, where he made a thorough analysis. He chose his words carefully and produced 169 sentences aimed at pressing the right "buttons" that would win him the support of the US people for a certain war strategy. Cicero's diatribes would pale beside his assumed posture. That day I had the impression I was listening to George W. Bush. His arguments were no different from the philosophy of his predecessor, except for a fig leaf: Obama opposed torture.

The main leader of the organization blamed for the terrorist act of 9/11 had been recruited and trained by the Central Intelligence Agency to fight the Soviet troops, even though he was not an Afghan.

Cuba's condemnation of the 9/11 terrorist acts and other additional measures were made public that same day. We also warned that the way to fight terrorism was not through war.

The organization of the Taliban—a word meaning "student"—sprang up from the Afghan forces fighting the Soviet Union; they were not enemies of the United States. An honest analysis would lead to the real story behind that war.

Today, it is not the Soviet troops but those of the United States and NATO that are occupying Afghanistan with great violence. The policy the new administration is offering the US people is the same as that of George W. Bush, who ordered the invasion of Iraq, a nation that had nothing to do with the attack on the Twin Towers.

The president of the United States is not saying a word about the hundreds of thousands of people, children and elderly people, who have perished in Iraq and Afghanistan or the millions of Iraqis and Afghans suffering the consequences of the war, even when they bear no responsibility whatsoever for the events in New York. Rather than a wish, the final phrase of his speech, "God bless America," sounded like an order to heaven.

Why did Obama accept the Nobel Peace Prize if he had already decided to fight the war in Afghanistan to the very end? His cynical action was uncalled for.

He announced later he would be receiving the prize in the Norwegian capital on December 11, and then travel on to the Copenhagen summit on December 18.

So now we should expect another dramatic speech in Oslo, a new compendium of phrases obscuring the reality of an imperial superpower with hundreds of military bases all over the world; 200 years of military interventions in our hemisphere; and over a century of genocidal actions in countries like Vietnam, Laos and elsewhere in Asia, Africa, the Middle East, the Balkans and other places on earth.

The problem now with Obama and his wealthy allies is that the planet they dominate with an iron fist is just falling apart.

The crime against humanity committed by Bush is well known, as he ignored the Kyoto Protocol and failed for 10 years to do what should have been done long before that. Obama is not ignorant. He is aware—as Gore was—of the grave danger threatening us all, but he hesitates and shows weakness vis-à-vis his country's blind and irresponsible oligarchy. He does not act like Lincoln did in 1861 to resolve the slavery issue and preserve national integrity, or like Roosevelt to cope with the economic crisis and the rise of fascism. On Tuesday, he merely cast a timid stone into the troubled waters of international opinion. The manager of the Environmental Protection Agency, Lisa Jackson, has stated that the threats to the US people's health and well-being posed by global warming make it possible for Obama to take action without consulting Congress.

None of the wars known to history pose a greater danger.

The wealthiest nations will try to place on the poorest the bulk of the burden to save the human species. The wealthiest should be asked to make the greatest sacrifices, be the most rational in the use of resources and bring a maximum of justice to human beings.

It is likely that in Copenhagen only minimal time will be bought to reach a binding agreement that can really help to find solutions. If that is the case, the summit might at least be considered a modest step forward.

Let's see what happens!

December 9, 2009

Humanity's Right to Life

Climate change is already causing enormous damage and hundreds of millions of poor people are enduring the consequences.

The most advanced research centers have claimed there is little time to avoid an irreversible catastrophe. James Hansen, from NASA's Goddard Institute, has said a proportion of 350 parts of carbon dioxide per million is still tolerable; however, the figure today is 390 and growing at a pace of two parts per million every year exceeding the levels of 600,000 years ago. Each one of the past two decades has been the warmest since the first records were taken, while carbon dioxide increased 80 parts per million in the past 150 years.

The melting of ice in the Arctic Sea and of the huge two-kilometer thick icecap covering Greenland; the melting of the South American glaciers feeding its main fresh water sources and the enormous volume covering the Antarctic; the melting of the remaining icecap on Kilimanjaro, the ice on the Himalayas and the large frozen area of Siberia are visible. Leading scientists fear abrupt quantitative changes in these natural phenomena that bring about the change.

Humanity entertained high hopes for the Copenhagen summit after the Kyoto Protocol signed in 1997 came into force in 2005. The resounding failure of the summit gave rise to shameful episodes that should be highlighted.

The United States, with less than 5 percent of the world population releases 25 percent of the carbon dioxide. The new US president had promised to cooperate with the international effort to tackle a new problem that afflicts that country as much as the rest of the world. In the meetings leading to the summit, it became clear that the leaders of the United States and the wealthiest countries were maneuvering to place the burden of sacrifice on the emerging and poor nations.

A great number of leaders and thousands of representatives of social movements and scientific institutions, determined to fight for the preservation of humanity from the greatest risk in history, converged on Copenhagen on the invitation of the organizers of the summit. I'd rather avoid referring to details of the brutality of the Danish police force against thousands of protesters and invitees from social and scientific movements who traveled to the Danish capital. I'll focus on the political features of the summit.

Actually, chaos prevailed in Copenhagen where incredible things happened. The social movements and scientific institutions were not allowed to attend the debates. There were heads of state and government who could not even express their views on crucial issues. Obama and the leaders of the wealthiest nations took over the conference, with the complicity of the Danish government. The UN agencies were pushed into the background.

Barack Obama, the last to arrive on the day of the summit for a 12-hour stay, met with two groups of invitees carefully chosen by him and his staff, and in the company of one of them met at the plenary hall with the rest of the high-level delegations. He made his remarks and left immediately through the back door. Except for the small group chosen by him, the other countries' representatives were prevented from taking the floor during that plenary session. The presidents of Bolivia and the Bolivarian Republic of Venezuela were allowed to speak because the chairman of the summit had no choice but to give them the floor in light of the strong pressure from those present.

In an adjacent room, Obama brought together the leaders of the wealthiest nations, some of the most important emerging states and two very poor countries. He then introduced a document, negotiated with two or three of the most important countries, ignored the UN

General Assembly, gave a press conference and left like Julius Caesar after one of his victorious wars in Asia Minor that prompted him to say: "I came, I saw, I conquered."

Even Gordon Brown, prime minister of the United Kingdom, said on October 19: "If we do not reach a deal over the next few months, let us be in no doubt, since once the damage from unchecked emissions growth is done, no retrospective global agreement at some future time can undo that choice. By then it will be irretrievably too late..."

Brown concluded his speech with these dramatic words: "We cannot afford to fail. If we fail now we will pay a heavy price. If we act now, if we act together, if we act with vision and resolve, success at Copenhagen is still within our reach, but, if we falter, the earth will itself be at risk and, for the planet, there is no Plan B."

Later he arrogantly remarked the United Nations could not be taken hostage by a group of countries like Cuba, Venezuela, Bolivia, Nicaragua and Tuvalu. At the same time, he accused China, India, Brazil, South Africa and other emerging countries of being lured by the United States into signing a document that throws the Kyoto Protocol in the wastebasket without a binding agreement involving the United States and its wealthy allies.

I find it necessary to remember how the United Nations was born hardly six decades ago, after the last world war, when there were no more than 50 independent countries. Today, after the hateful colonial system has ceased to exist, thanks to the resolute struggle of the peoples, it has a membership of over 190 independent nations. For many years, even the People's Republic of China was denied admission to the UN while a puppet regime was its representative in that institution and in the privileged Security Council.

The resolute support of the growing number of Third World nations would prove indispensable to China's international recognition and become an extremely significant element in winning the acceptance of China's rights at the UN by the United States and its NATO allies.

It was the Soviet Union that made the greatest contribution to the heroic fight against fascism. More than 25 million of its people perished while the country was terribly devastated. It was from that struggle that it emerged as a superpower with the capacity to partly balance the absolute domination of the US imperial system and the former colonial powers to plunder the Third World countries at will. Following the demise of the Soviet Union, the United States extended its political and military power to the East—right up to Russia's heart—and enhanced its influence in the rest of Europe. Therefore, what happened in Copenhagen came as no surprise.

I want to stress how unfair and outrageous were the UK prime minister's remarks and the Yankees' attempt to impose as the summit accord a document that was at no time discussed with the participating countries.

During his press conference on December 21, Cuba's Foreign Minister Bruno Rodríguez said something undeniable. I will quote him:

> "I would like to emphasize that no agreement of the Conference of the Parties was reached in Copenhagen, that no decision was made as to binding or nonbinding commitments or pertaining to International Law; that simply did not happen. There was no agreement in Copenhagen.
>
> "The summit was a failure and a deception for the world… the lack of political will was exposed… [I]t was a step backward in the actions of the international community to prevent or mitigate the effects of climate change…
>
> "[T]he average world temperature could rise by 5 degrees…"

Then our foreign minister noted other interesting facts on the likely consequences of climate change according to the latest scientific research:

> "From the Kyoto Protocol to today the developed countries' emissions rose by 12.8 percent... and 55 percent of that volume belongs to the United States.

> "The average annual consumption of oil is 25 barrels for an American, 11 barrels for a European, less than two barrels for a Chinese and less than one barrel for a Latin American or Caribbean citizen.
>
> "Thirty countries, including those of the European Union, are consuming 80 percent of the fuel produced."

The fact is that the developed countries that signed the Kyoto Protocol have dramatically increased their emissions. Now they want to replace the adopted bases of the emissions from 1990 with those of 2005. This means that the United States, which is the main source of emissions, would be reducing its emissions of 25 years ago by only 3 percent. This is a shameful mockery of world public opinion.

The Cuban foreign minister, speaking on behalf of a group of ALBA member countries, defended China, India, Brazil, South Africa and other important economically emerging states. He stressed the principle adopted in Kyoto that "common but differentiated responsibilities" means "the responsibility of the historical accumulators and the developed countries, who are the culprits in this catastrophe, differs from that of the small island states and the South countries, above all, the least developed...

> "Responsibility means financing; responsibility means technology transfer on appropriate terms. But, at this point, Obama resorts to a word game and instead of referring to 'common but differentiated responsibilities,' he speaks of 'common but differentiated responses.'
>
> "[Obama] then leaves the plenary hall without taking the trouble of listening to anybody; no had he listened to anybody before taking the floor."

In a subsequent press conference, before departing from the Danish capital, Obama said: "There has been a meaningful and unprecedented breakthrough here in Copenhagen. For the first time in history, the largest economies have come to jointly accept responsibility."

In his clear and irrefutable presentation, our foreign minister asked: "What does it mean that 'the largest economies have come to jointly accept responsibility'? It means they are placing a large part of the burden of financing the relief and adaptation to climate change on countries mostly of the South, on China, Brazil, India and South Africa. Because it must be said that in Copenhagen we witnessed an assault, an obstruction against China, Brazil, India and South Africa, and against every other euphemistically labeled developing country."

These were the resounding and incontestable words our foreign minister used to describe what happened in Copenhagen.

I must add that, when at 10:00 a.m. on December 19 our Vice-President Esteban Lazo and the Cuban foreign minister had already left, a belated attempt was made to resurrect the Copenhagen cadaver with a summit accord. At that moment, practically every head of state had departed and there were hardly any ministers around. Again, the denunciation by the remaining members of the delegations from Cuba, Venezuela, Bolivia, Nicaragua and other countries defeated the maneuver. That was the end of the inglorious summit.

Another fact that should not be overlooked is that at the most critical moment of that day, in the wee small hours, the Cuban foreign minister, together with the delegations waging an honorable battle, offered UN Secretary General Ban Ki-Moon their cooperation in the increasingly difficult struggle being fought as well as in future efforts necessary to preserve the life of our species.

The environmental group World Wildlife Fund has warned that if emissions are not drastically reduced climate change will go unchecked in the next five to 10 years.

But there is no need to prove what is said here about what Obama did [in Copenhagen]. The US president stated on Wednesday December 23 that people are justified in being disappointed with the outcome of the UN summit on climate change. In an interview with the CBS television network, the president said, "instead of a total collapse if nothing had been done, which would have been a huge step backward, at least we could remain more or less where we were..."

According to the press dispatch, Obama is the target of most of the criticism from the countries that almost unanimously feel that the result of the summit was a disaster.

The UN is now in a quandary since many countries would find it humiliating to ask others to adhere to the arrogant and antidemocratic accord.

The only way to proceed, in my opinion, is to carry on with the battle and to demand in every meeting, particularly in those in Bonn and Mexico, humanity's right to life, with the morale and the strength that the truth gives us.

December 26, 2009

Health Care Reform in the United States

Barack Obama is a fanatical believer in the imperialist capitalist system imposed by the United States on the world. He ends his speeches with "God bless the United States."

Some of his actions have wounded the sensibility of world opinion, which viewed with sympathy the African-American candidate's victory over that country's extreme right-wing candidate. Basing himself on one of the worst economic crises the world has seen, and the pain caused by young Americans who have lost their lives or have been injured or mutilated in his predecessor's genocidal wars of conquest, he won the votes of the majority of 50 percent of Americans who deign to go to the polls in that democratic country.

Out of an elemental sense of ethics, Obama should have abstained from accepting the Nobel Peace Prize when he had already decided to send 40,000 soldiers to an absurd war in the heart of Asia.

The current administration's militarist policies, its plunder of natural resources and unequal exchange with the poor countries of the Third World are in no way different from those of its predecessors, almost all of them extremely right wing, with some exceptions, throughout the past century.

At the Copenhagen summit an antidemocratic document was imposed on the international community, which had believed [Obama's] promise to cooperate in the fight against climate change; this was another act that disappointed many people in the world. The United States, the largest emitter of greenhouse gases, was not willing to make the necessary sacrifices, despite the sweet words of its president beforehand.

It would be interminable to list the contradictions between the ideas that the Cuban nation has defended at great sacrifice for half a century and the egotistical policies of that colossal empire.

Nevertheless, we harbor no antagonism toward Obama, much less toward the US people. We believe that health reform has been an important battle and a success for his government. It would seem, however, to be something truly unusual, 234 years after the Declaration of Independence in Philadelphia in 1776, inspired by the ideas of the French encyclopedists, that the US government has passed [a law for] medical attention for the vast majority of its citizens, something that Cuba achieved for its entire population half a century ago, despite the cruel and inhumane blockade imposed and still in effect by the most powerful country that ever existed. Before that, after almost half a century of independence and after a bloody war, Abraham Lincoln was able to attain legal freedom for slaves.

On the other hand, I cannot stop thinking about a world in which more than one-third of the population lacks the medical attention and medicines essential to ensuring its health. This situation will be aggravated as climate change and water and food scarcity increase in a globalized world, a world in which the population is growing, forests are disappearing, agricultural land is diminishing, the air is becoming unbreathable. The human species that emerged less than 200,000 years ago—in other words, 3.5 million years after the first forms of life emerged on the planet—is running the real risk of disappearing.

Accepting that health reform signifies a success for his government, the current US president cannot ignore that climate change is a threat to the health, and even worse, to the very existence of all the world's nations, when the increase in temperature—beyond the critical limits that are in sight—is melting the frozen waters of the glaciers, and the tens of millions of cubic kilometers stored in the enormous ice caps in the Antarctic, Greenland and Siberia will have melted within a few dozen years, leaving underwater all of the world's port facilities and the lands where a large part of the global population now lives, feeds itself and works.

Obama, the leaders of the free countries and their allies, their scientists and their sophisticated research centers know this; it is impossible for them not to know it.

I understand the satisfaction in the president's speech expressing and recognizing the contributions of members of Congress and the administration who made possible the miracle of health reform, which strengthens the government's position vis-à-vis the lobbyists and political mercenaries who are impeding the administration. It would be worse if those who engaged in torture, hired assassins and genocide should reoccupy the US government. As a person who is unquestionably intelligent and sufficiently well-informed, Obama knows I am not exaggerating. I hope that the ridiculous remarks he sometimes makes about Cuba are not clouding his intelligence.

In the wake of the success in this battle for the right to health care for all Americans, 12 million immigrants, in their immense majority Latin American, Haitian and from other Caribbean countries, are demanding the legalization of their presence in the United States, where they do the hardest jobs that US society could not do without, where they are arrested, separated from their families and sent back to their countries.

The vast majority of them immigrated to North America as a consequence of the dictatorships imposed in the region by the United States, and the brutal policy to which they have been subjected as a result of the plunder of their resources and unequal trade. Their family remittances constitute a large percentage of the GDP of their economies. They are now hoping for an act of elemental justice. When an Adjustment Act was imposed on the Cuban people, promoting brain drain and the loss of its educated young people, why are such brutal methods used against illegal immigrants from Latin American and Caribbean countries?

The devastating earthquake that lashed Haiti—the poorest country in Latin America, which has just suffered an unprecedented natural disaster that involved the death of more than 200,000 people—and the terrible economic damage that a similar phenomenon has caused in Chile, are eloquent evidence of the dangers that threaten so-called civilization, and the need for drastic measures that can give the human species hope of survival.

The Cold War did not bring any benefits to the world's peoples. The immense economic, technological and scientific power of the United States would not survive the tragedy that is hovering over the planet. President Obama should check out the pertinent information on his computer and converse with his most eminent scientists; he will see how far his country is from being the model for humanity he extols.

Because he is an African American, he suffered the affronts of discrimination, as he relates in his book, *The Dreams of My Father*; he knew about the poverty in which tens of millions of Americans live; he was educated, but he also enjoyed, as a successful professional, the privileges of the life of the rich middle class, and he ended up idealizing the social system that—with the economic crisis, the uselessly sacrificed lives of Americans and his unquestionable political talent—gave him his electoral victory.

Nevertheless, the most recalcitrant right-wing forces see Obama as an extremist, and are threatening him by continuing to do battle in the Senate to neutralize the effects of the health reform, and openly sabotaging him in various states of the Union, declaring the new law unconstitutional.

The problems of our era are even far more serious.

The International Monetary Fund, the World Bank and other international credit agencies, under the strict control of the United States, are allowing the large US banks—the creators of fiscal paradises and responsible for the financial chaos on the planet—to be kept afloat by the government in every one of the system's frequent and growing crises.

At its whim, the US Federal Reserve issues the convertible currency that pays for the wars of conquest, the profits of the military industrial complex, the military bases distributed throughout the world and the large investments with which transnationals control the economy in many countries in the world. Nixon unilaterally suspended the conversion of the dollar into gold, while the vaults of the banks in New York hold 7,000 tons of gold, something more than 25 percent of the world's reserves of this metal, a figure which at the end of World War II stood at more than 80 percent. It is argued that the [US] public debt exceeds $10 trillion, more than 70 percent of its GDP, a burden that will be passed on to coming generations. This is affirmed when, in reality, it is the world economy that pays this debt with the huge spending on goods and services that it provides to acquire US dollars, with which the large US transnationals have taken over a considerable part of the world's wealth, and which sustain that nation's consumer society.

Anyone can see that such a system is unsustainable and why the wealthiest sectors in the United States and its allies in the world defend a system sustained only by ignorance, lies and conditioned reflexes sown via a monopoly of the mass media, including the principal Internet networks.

Today, the structure is collapsing in the face of the accelerated advance of climate change and its disastrous consequences, which are placing humanity in an exceptional dilemma.

Wars among the powers no longer seem to be the solution to major contradictions as they were until the second half of the 20th century, but are now affecting the factors that make human survival possible to such an extent that they could bring the existence of the current intelligent species inhabiting our planet to a premature end.

A few days ago, I expressed my conviction, in the light of dominant scientific knowledge today, that human beings have to solve their problems on planet Earth, given that they will never be able to cover the distance that separates the sun from the closest star (located four light years away, a speed that is equivalent to 300,000 kilometers per second) even if there was a planet similar to our beautiful Earth in the vicinity of the sun.

The United States is investing fabulous sums to discover if there is water on the planet Mars, and whether some elemental form of life existed or exists there. Nobody knows why, unless it is out of pure scientific curiosity. Millions of species on our planet are disappearing at an increasing rate and its fabulous volumes of water are constantly being poisoned.

The new laws of science—based on Einstein's theories on energy and matter and the Big Bang theory as the origin of the millions of constellations and infinite stars or other hypotheses—have given way to profound changes in fundamental concepts of space and time that are occupying theologians' attention. One of them, our Brazilian friend Frei Betto, discusses the issue in his book *La obra del artista: una vision holística del Universe* (The Artist's Work: A Holistic View of the Universe), launched at the last International Book Fair in Havana.

Scientific advances in the last 100 years have impacted on traditional views that prevailed for thousands of years in the social sciences and even in philosophy and theology.

The interest that most honest thinkers are taking in this new knowledge is notable, but we know absolutely nothing of President Obama's thinking on the compatibility of consumer societies with science.

Meanwhile, it is worthwhile, now and then, to devote time to meditating on these issues. Certainly human beings will not cease to dream and approach things with serenity and nerves of steel. This is a duty—at least for those who chose the profession of politics and made a noble and crucial commitment to a human society of solidarity and justice.

March 24, 2010

The Insanities of Our Times

We have no choice but to call things by their right names. Those who still have an ounce of common sense find it easy to see how little realism is left in today's world.

When US President Barack Obama was nominated for the Nobel Peace Prize, Michael Moore said, "Now, earn it!" Many people liked the smart remark; it was a clever phrase, even though many considered the decision by the Norwegian committee an example of demagoguery and an exaltation of the apparently inoffensive politicking of the new US president, an African American, a good communicator and a clever politician at the head of a powerful empire in the midst of a deep economic crisis.

The world conference in Copenhagen was about to be held and Obama sparked hopes that the United States would join the world consensus in favor of a binding agreement to prevent the ecological catastrophe threatening the human species. What happened there was disappointing; the international public had become the victim of a painful deception.

At the recent World Conference of the Peoples on Climate Change and the Rights of Mother Earth held in Bolivia responses were offered reflecting the wisdom of the ancient indigenous nations, invaded and virtually devastated by the European conquerors who, in search of gold and easy wealth, for centuries imposed their selfish cultures that are incompatible with the most sacred interests of humankind.

Two news reports received yesterday expressed the empire's philosophy that tries to make us believe in its "democratic, peaceful, selfless and honest" nature. Just read the text of these press dispatches dated in the US capital.

> "WASHINGTON, April 22, 2010. In coming years, President Barack Obama will decide whether to deploy a new class of weapons capable of reaching any corner of the earth from the United States in under an hour with such accuracy and force that they would greatly diminish America's reliance on its nuclear arsenal."

Although this new super-bomb, to be delivered by Minuteman missiles, will not carry nuclear warheads their destructive capability will be similar, as confirmed by the fact that its deployment is foreshadowed in the recently signed START 2 agreements with Russia. The Moscow authorities demanded, and managed to include in the agreement, that the United States remove one of its nuclear warheads for each one of these missiles.

According to reports in the *New York Times* and the CBS TV network, these new bombs, known as Prompt Global Strike (PGS) would be able to kill Al Qaeda leader Osama Bin Laden in a cave in Afghanistan, destroy a North Korean missile being prepared for launch or attack an Iranian nuclear site, "all without crossing the nuclear threshold."

The advantage of having the military option of a non-nuclear weapon with the same effect as the targeted impact of a nuclear bomb is considered interesting by the Obama administration. The project had been initially undertaken by Obama's predecessor, Republican President George W. Bush, but it was blocked by protests from Moscow. The Russian authorities had said that, given the Minuteman's capability to deliver nuclear warheads, it was impossible to determine whether the launching of a PGS did not mark the beginning of a nuclear attack.

However, the Obama administration feels that it can give Russia and China the necessary guarantees to avoid misunderstandings. The missile silos of the new weapon will be installed in areas away from the nuclear warhead depots and they can be regularly supervised by experts from Moscow or Beijing.

The super-bomb could be delivered by a Minuteman missile capable of flying through the atmosphere at several times the sound of speed while carrying 1,000 pounds of explosives. Then, extremely sophisticated equipment will enable the missile to release the bomb letting it fall with great accuracy on the selected targets.

Responsibility for the PGS project—at an estimated cost of $250 million in only its first experimental year—fell on General Kevin Chilton, commander of the US nuclear arsenal. Chilton explained that the PGS will fill a gap in the range of options currently available to the Pentagon.

"Today," he said, "we can present some conventional options to the president to strike a target anywhere on the globe that range from 96 hours to... maybe four, five, six hours." For a faster action, he conceded, there is only a nuclear response.

With this new bomb, in the future the United States could act quickly and with conventional resources both against a terrorist group or an enemy country, in a much shorter time and avoiding international outrage over the use of nuclear weapons.

It is planned to start testing in 2014 and to have it available in the US arsenal by 2017. Obama will no longer be in power but this super-bomb will be the non-nuclear legacy of this president who has already been awarded the Nobel Peace Prize.

> "Washington April 23, 2010. A US Air Force unmanned spacecraft has blasted off from Florida, amid a veil of secrecy about its military mission.
>
> "The robotic space plane, or X-37B, lifted off from Cape Canaveral atop an Atlas V rocket at 7:52pm local time on Thursday (0952 AEST on Friday), according video released by the military.
>
> " 'The launch is a go,' Air Force Major Angie Blair told AFP.

"Resembling a miniature space shuttle, the plane is 8.9 meters long and has a wing-span of 4.5 meters.

"The reusable space vehicle has been years in the making and the military has offered only vague explanations as to its purpose or role in the American military's arsenal.

" 'The vehicle is designed to 'provide an "on-orbit laboratory" test environment to prove new technology and components before those technologies are committed to operational satellite programs,' the Air Force said in a recent release.

"Officials said the X-37B would eventually return for a landing at Vandenberg Air Force Base in California, but did not say how long the inaugural mission would last.

" 'In all honesty, we don't know when it's coming back,' Gary Payton, deputy undersecretary for Air Force space programs, told reporters in a conference call this week.

"Payton said the plane could stay in space for up to nine months.

"The space plane—manufactured by Boeing—began as a project of NASA in 1999, and was eventually handed over to the US Air Force Rapid Capabilities Office.

"The Air Force has plans for a second X-37B, scheduled to launch in 2011."

What else do they need?

Today they face an enormous obstacle: already unstoppable climate change. There is talk of the unavoidable rise of temperature by more than two degrees centigrade, with catastrophic consequences. Within only 40 years, the world population will increase by 2 billion to reach the figure of 9 billion people. Harbors, hotels, tourist resorts, roads, industries and facilities close to the ports will be underwater in less than half the lifetime of those from wealthy and developed nations, the same nations that today selfishly refuse to make the least sacrifices to ensure the survival of the human species. Farmland and drinking water will be considerably reduced. The oceans will be polluted and many marine species will no longer be edible while others will be extinct. This is not simple logic but the result of scientific research.

Through natural genetics and the migration of various species from one continent to another, human beings have been able to increase food and other yields per hectare. Thus, for some time, humanity has suffered less from the shortage of food such as maize, potato, wheat, fiber and other essential products. Later, genetic manipulation and the use of chemical fertilizers also contributed to solving crucial needs but they, too, are coming to the end of their possibilities to produce healthy food for human consumption.

On the other hand, we are witnessing the depletion in barely two centuries of the hydrocarbons that took nature 400 million years to create. Likewise, crucial nonrenewable mineral resources required by the world economy are being depleted. At the same time, science has created the capacity to destroy the planet several times over in a matter of hours. The major contradiction of our times is precisely the capacity of the human species for self-destruction and its inability to govern itself.

Human beings have managed to raise their possibilities for life that exceeds their own capacity to survive, and in this battle they are consuming resources at an accelerated pace. Science has made it possible to turn matter into energy, as in the case of nuclear reaction—through large investments—but there is no sign that turning energy into matter is even viable. The infinite cost of investments in the relevant research is showing the impossibility of achieving in a few decades what it took the universe tens of thousands of millions of years to create. Will it be necessary for Barack Obama, the wunderkind, to explain this to us? Science has experienced remarkable growth but ignorance and poverty are also growing. Can anyone demonstrate the opposite?

April 26, 2010

The Empire and the War

Two days ago, I said in a few words that imperialism was unable to solve the extremely serious problem of drug abuse, which has become a scourge for people all over the world. Today, I wish to deal with another issue I consider of major significance.

The current danger that the United States attacks North Korea, following the recent incident in the territorial waters of the latter, could perhaps be thwarted if the president of the People's Republic of China decides to exercise the right of veto—a prerogative that country totally dislikes—with respect to the agreements currently under discussion at the UN Security Council.

But, there is a second and more serious problem for which the United States has no possible answer; this is the conflict with Iran. This could clearly be seen coming ever since President Barack Obama made his speech at the Islamic University of Al-Azhar in Cairo on June 4, 2009.

In a "Reflection" I wrote only four days later, when I had access to an official copy of his remarks, I used many parts of his speech to analyze its significance. I will now quote some of Obama's remarks:

> "We meet at a time of tension between the United States and Muslims around the World..."
>
> "...colonialism... denied rights and opportunities to many Muslims, and [during] Cold War... Muslim-majority countries were too often treated as proxies without regard to their own aspirations."

This and other arguments sounded particularly impressive as they were voiced by an African-American US president; they resonated like the self-evident truths contained in the Declaration of Independence in Philadelphia, July 4, 1776.

> "I have come here [to Cairo] to seek a new beginning between the United States and Muslims around the world; one based upon mutual interest and mutual respect...
>
> "As the Holy Koran tells us, 'Be conscious of God and speak always the truth.'
>
> "And I consider it part of my responsibility as president of the United States to fight against negative stereotypes of Islam wherever they appear....

Thus, he continued dealing with thorny issues from the universe of insoluble contradictions involving US policies.

> "In the middle of the Cold War, the United States played a role in the overthrow of a democratically elected Iranian government. Since the Islamic revolution, Iran has played a role in acts of hostage-taking and violence against US troops and civilians...."
>
> "America's strong bonds with Israel are well known. This bond is unbreakable...."
>
> "Many wait in refugee camps in the West Bank, Gaza and neighboring lands for a life of peace and security that they have never been able to lead."

Today, we know that white phosphorus and other inhumane and cruel substances are often dropped on the population of the Gaza Strip in a truly Nazi-like fascist frenzy. Nevertheless, Obama's assertions seemed animated and on occasion sincere as he repeated them again during his feverish race around the world in his US Air Force One.

Yesterday, May 31, the international community was shocked when in international waters, tens of thousands of miles off the coast of Gaza, nearly 100 Israeli paratroops jumped from helicopters, in the wee small hours, recklessly firing on hundreds of peaceful people of various nationalities, causing—according to press reports—no less than 20 dead and scores of injured. There were also Americans among those under attack, who were carrying goods to the Palestinians besieged in their own homeland.

When Obama spoke at the Islamic University of Al-Azhar about "the overthrow of a democratically elected Iranian government" and immediately added that "since the Islamic revolution, Iran has played a role in acts of hostage-taking and violence against US troops and civilians," he was referring to the revolutionary movement promoted by Ayatollah Ruhollah Khomeini who, from Paris and without a single weapon, crushed the armed forces of the most powerful US gendarme in South Asia. It was very difficult for the mightiest power of the world not to succumb to the temptation of setting up one of its military bases there, south of the Soviet Union.

More than five decades before, the United States had subdued another absolutely democratic revolution when it overthrew the Iranian government headed by Mohammad Mossadegh, who had been elected prime minister of Iran on April 24, 1951. On May 1 that same year, the Iranian Senate approved the nationalization of oil, which had been the main demand during the struggle. "So far, our long years of negotiations with foreign countries have proven unsuccessful," Mossadegh stated.

He obviously meant the big capitalist powers that controlled the world economy. In view of the intransigence of British Petroleum, then known as the Anglo-Iranian Oil Company, Iran seized its facilities.

The country was unable to train its own technicians. The United Kingdom had withdrawn its skilled personnel and imposed a blockade on spare parts and markets. It had also sent the Royal Navy ready for action against that country. As a result, Iran's oil production decreased from 241.4 million barrels in 1952 to 10.6 million in 1953. In such favorable conditions, the CIA organized the coup d'état that ousted Mossadegh, who passed away three years later. The monarchy was then reinstated and a firm US ally took power in Iran.

That is the only thing the United States has done with other nations. Ever since the creation of that country on the richest soils of the planet, it never respected the rights of the indigenous population who had lived there for thousands of years or of those brought in as slaves by the English colonizers.

Nevertheless, I am sure that millions of intelligent and honest Americans understand these truths.

President Obama can make hundreds of speeches trying to accommodate irreconcilable contradictions to the detriment of the truth; or he can believe in the spell woven by his well-articulated words while making concessions to unethical people and groups. He can also describe fantastic worlds that exist only in his head, planted there by unscrupulous advisors aware of his tendencies.

Two unavoidable questions: Will Obama be able to enjoy the excitement of a second presidential term without seeing the Pentagon or the State of Israel, whose behavior shows that it does not accept US decisions, use their nuclear weapons on Iran? What will life on our planet be like after that?

June 1, 2010

Obama's Speech in Arizona

Yesterday I listened to Obama when he spoke at the University of Tucson where homage was being paid to the six people murdered and the 14 wounded in the Arizona massacre [January 8, 2011], especially the Democratic congresswoman for that state [Gabrielle Giffords], seriously wounded by a gunshot to the head.

It was the deed of an unbalanced person, drunk on the preaching of hatred that reigns in US society, where the fascist Tea Party has imposed its extremism on the Republican Party which, under the aegis of George W. Bush, led the world to where it is now, on the brink of the abyss.

Added to the disaster of wars has been the greatest economic crisis in the history of the United States and a government debt that today is equal to 100 percent of the GDP, together with a monthly deficit totaling more than $80 billion and more homes being lost as a result of unpaid mortgages. The prices of oil, metals, and food are progressively going up. The lack of confidence in paper currency causes gold purchases to increase and there are quite a few people who see the price of gold increasing to $2,000 an ounce. There are some who think it will go as high as $2,500.

Climatic conditions have worsened, with considerable losses registered in the harvests in the Russian Federation, Europe, China, Australia, North and South America and in other areas, endangering the food supplies of more than 80 Third World countries, creating political instability in a growing number of them.

The world is facing so many political, military, energy, food and environmental problems that no country wants the United States to return to extremist positions that could increase the risk of nuclear war.

International condemnation of the crime in Arizona was almost unanimous, a crime that was an expression of extremism. No one expected the president of the United States to make an impassioned or confrontational speech, something that wouldn't be consistent with his style or with the domestic circumstances and the climate of irrational hatred that prevails in the United States.

The victims of the shooting were undoubtedly brave, each with their merit, and most were humble citizens; if that was not the case, they wouldn't have been there, defending the right of all US citizens to medical care and opposing the anti-immigrant laws.

The mother of a nine-year-old girl born on September 11 had stated courageously that the hatred unleashed in the world had to cease. I have no doubt that the victims were worthy of recognition by the US, along with the citizens of Tucson, the students at the university and the doctors who, whenever events of this type occur, always unreservedly show natural human solidarity. The severely wounded congresswoman, Gabrielle Giffords, deserves the national and international accolade she has received. Today, the medical team was continuing to give positive reports on the state of her condition.

Of course, Obama's speech lacked the moral condemnation of the policies that inspired such an act.

I was trying to imagine how men such as Franklin Delano Roosevelt would have acted in similar circumstances, not to mention Lincoln, who didn't shrink from giving his famous Gettysburg Address. What other moment is the US president waiting for to express the opinion that I am sure is shared by the great majority of those in the United States?

It is not a matter of the US government lacking an exceptional personality to lead it. What transforms a president into a historic figure, who has been able to reach that position because of their merits, does not lie in the individual, but in the need for that person to play a role at a particular moment in the history of their nation.

When Obama began his speech yesterday, he looked tense and very much dependent on the written pages. He soon recovered his calm, his usual command of the stage, and the precise words to express his ideas. What he didn't say was because he didn't want to say it.

For delivery of well-written remarks and just praise for those deserving it, he could be awarded a prize.

For a political speech, he left a lot to be desired.

January 13, 2011

The "State of The Union" Address

After his January 12, [2011], address at the University of Tucson, Arizona, on the massacre that had taken place four days earlier, people waited with interest for the US president's speech on this same topic. Six people died and 14 were injured, including young Democratic congresswoman Gabrielle Giffords, who was elected to the US Congress for the third time and who had been opposed to the anti-immigration laws in Arizona, a state that was part of the territory snatched from Mexico in the unjust war of 1848.

The Tea Party, the right-wing fascist element of the Republican Party, gained a notable victory among those who bothered to vote in the elections. The people of Arizona, as in the rest of the United States, reacted with outrage. This reaction was without a doubt correct, and that is what I have said.

I have never doubted the ethics that the people show, independent of the policy of their governments.

If that speech by Obama was lacking, in terms of addressing the incredible primitivism reflected in the widespread and practically unrestricted use of lethal firearms, his [January 25, 2011] State of the Union address deserves an ethical and political analysis because of the fact that, independent of the president and the congress, the United States is a superpower whose actions profoundly affect the entire human species.

No country on its own should look for, or can come up, with answers to the problems that the world faces today.

First, Obama is engulfed in an electoral process. He has to speak for both the Democrats and Republicans, those who vote, those who don't vote, multimillionaires and beggars, Protestants and Catholics, Christians and Muslims, believers and nonbelievers, blacks and whites, those who support stem cell research and those who don't support it, homosexuals and heterosexuals, every citizen and their counterpart, to conclude by saying that they are all Americans, as if the remaining 95.5 percent, or 6.9 billion inhabitants on the rest of the planet did not exist.

Obama dives into this subject on the first pages of his address that lasted an hour:

> "At stake right now is not who wins the next election... At stake is whether new jobs and industries take root in this country or somewhere else... It is whether we sustain the leadership that has made America not just a place on a map, but the light to the world.
>
> "We are poised for progress... the stock market has come roaring back. Corporate profits are up. The economy is growing again."

Immediately following these words, Obama tried to move us with a passage that seems to be taken straight from a US movie that my generation will remember, "Gone with the Wind," about the terrible civil war between the industrialized north and the agrarian and slave-holding south, during the time of the exceptional leader, Abraham Lincoln.

> "That world has changed. And for many, the change has been painful. I've seen it in the shuttered windows of once booming factories, and the vacant storefronts on once busy Main Streets. I've heard it in the frustrations of Americans who've seen their paychecks dwindle or their jobs disappear—proud men and women who feel like the rules have been changed in the middle of the game...
>
> "Steel mills that once needed 1,000 workers can now do the same work with 100... Meanwhile, nations like China and India realized that with some changes of their own, they could compete in this new world...

Just recently, China became the home to the world's largest private solar research facility, and the world's fastest computer…

"America still has the largest, most prosperous economy in the world…

"We know what it takes to compete for the jobs and industries of our time. We need to out-innovate, out-educate, and out-build the rest of the world. We have to make America the best place on Earth to do business… And tonight, I'd like to talk about how we get there."

Obama never talks about the big monopoly businesses that today control and plunder the planet's resources. He never mentions the [1944] Bretton Woods accord, the system imposed on a world in ruins because of war, where the United States took control of the financial institutions and the International Monetary Fund, where they fiercely hold on to veto power. He never says one word about the colossal con by Nixon in 1971 when he unilaterally suspended the conversion of the dollar to gold, printed US dollars without any sort of limit, and acquired innumerable goods and riches in the world, for which he primarily paid with paper, whose value over 40 years has fallen to 2.5 percent of what it was worth then.

On the other hand, Obama likes to tell poetic tales about small businesses supposedly to dazzle, captivate and move the audience who are not warned about the reality. His speech, style and tone all seem designed to have the audience listen, like well-behaved children, to his moving stories.

"Robert and Gary Allen are brothers who run a small Michigan roofing company. After September 11, they volunteered their best roofers to help repair the Pentagon. But half of their factory went unused, and the recession hit them hard. Today, with the help of a government loan, that empty space is being used to manufacture solar shingles that are being sold all across the country. In Robert's words, 'We reinvented ourselves.'…

"We're issuing a challenge. We're telling America's scientists and engineers that if they assemble teams of the best minds in their fields,

> and focus on the hardest problems in clean energy, we'll fund the Apollo projects of our time."

Then, without a pause, he took our breath away:

> "At the California Institute of Technology, they're developing a way to turn sunlight and water into fuel for our cars."

The planet has been saved! Or, at least, it won't perish due to an excess of CO^2 or for lack of energy. It reminds me of something that happened over 40 years ago when a group of enterprising young Cuban scientists spoke to me with great enthusiasm about this same idea, based on theoretical principles. My blind faith in science led me to find everything they asked for, including an isolated facility where they would work for years with such enthusiasm that even when a motor blew up and almost killed some of them, they continued their research.

I'm not denying anything, and much less a great Californian institute, but please, Mr. President, share this information with the world so that other scientists can work on this same project. This is not a matter of profit, as humanity would be prepared to pay anything your scientists want, and I am almost sure that even Michael Moore would applaud if you then received 10 Nobel prizes.

After another encouraging comment about the Oak Ridge National Laboratory and supercomputers installed so that nuclear plants can produce more energy, the president assured us: "With more research and incentives, we can break our dependence on oil with biofuel, and become the first country to have one million electric vehicles on the road by 2015."

Unperturbed, the president continued:

> "Think about it. Over the next 10 years, nearly half of all new jobs will require education that goes beyond a high school education. And yet, as many as a quarter of our students aren't even finishing high school.

> The quality of our math and science education lags behind many other nations. America has fallen to ninth in the proportion of young people with a college degree. And so the question is whether all of us—as citizens, and as parents—are willing to do what's necessary to give every child a chance to succeed…
>
> "[W]e will reach the goal that I set two years ago: By the end of the decade, America will once again have the highest proportion of college graduates in the world…
>
> "Others come here from abroad to study in our colleges and universities. But as soon as they obtain advanced degrees, we send them back home to compete against us. It makes no sense."

Of course, we are expected to excuse this promotion of the brain drain, which our friend Obama has no interest in trying to hide, we must excuse him given his passion for science and healthy competition.

> "The third step in winning the future is rebuilding America. To attract new businesses to our shores, we need the fastest, most reliable ways to move people, goods, and information—from high-speed rail to high-speed Internet.
>
> "Our infrastructure used to be the best, but our lead has slipped. South Korean homes now have greater Internet access than we do. Countries in Europe and Russia invest more in their roads and railways than we do. China is building faster trains and newer airports…
>
> "So over the last two years, we've begun rebuilding for the 21st century, a project that has meant thousands of good jobs for the hard-hit construction industry. And tonight, I'm proposing that we redouble those efforts…
>
> "Within 25 years, our goal is to give 80 percent of Americans access to high-speed rail…
>
> "Within the next five years, we'll make it possible for businesses to deploy the next generation of high-speed wireless coverage to 98 percent of all Americans… [This is] about a rural community in Iowa or Alabama where farmers and small business owners will be able to sell their products all over the world…
>
> "[T]his will make America a better place to do business and create jobs."

"[A] parade of lobbyists has rigged the tax code to benefit particular companies and industries...

"To help businesses sell more products abroad, we set a goal of doubling our exports by 2014—because the more we export, the more jobs we create here at home... Recently, we signed agreements with India and China that will support more than 250,000 jobs here in the United States."

"Before I took office, I made it clear... that I would only sign deals that keep faith with American workers and promote American jobs... and that's what I intend to do as we pursue agreements with Panama and Colombia..."

Some of the things Obama talked about give an idea of the dramatic consequences endured by the poorest sectors in his own country in the midst of the 21st century. For example, he said:

"I'm not willing to tell James Howard, a brain cancer patient from Texas, that his treatment might not be covered...

"We are living with a legacy of deficit spending that began almost a decade ago. And in the wake of the financial crisis, some of that was necessary to keep credit flowing, save jobs, and put money in people's pockets... So tonight, I am proposing that starting this year, we freeze annual domestic spending for the next five years...

"The Secretary of Defense has also agreed to cut tens of billions of dollars in spending that he and his generals believe our military can do without...

"And if we truly care about our deficit, we simply can't afford a permanent extension of the tax cuts for the wealthiest 2 percent of Americans. Before we take money away from our schools or scholarships away from our students, we should ask millionaires to give up their tax break...

"Because you deserve to know when your elected officials are meeting with lobbyists, I ask Congress to do what the White House has already done—put that information online."

I think the mere presence of an army of lobbyists working and negotiating with members of Congress is a shameful fact for any civilized country. "America's moral example must always shine for all who yearn for freedom and justice and dignity," Mr. Obama tells us, and immediately moves on to another theme. "Look to Iraq, where nearly 100,000 of our brave men and women have left with their heads held high."

Mission accomplished! I remembered.

> "Because Republicans and Democrats approved the new START treaty, far fewer nuclear weapons and launchers will be deployed…
>
> "Because of a diplomatic effort to insist that Iran meet its obligations, the Iranian government now faces tougher sanctions, tighter sanctions than ever before. And on the Korean Peninsula, we stand with our ally South Korea, and insist that North Korea keeps its commitment to abandon nuclear weapons."

The president, as I observed, did not mention a single word about the selective assassination of Iranian scientists by the intelligence agencies of the United States and its allies, about which he was well informed.

Instead, he expanded on his remarks saying:

> "This is just a part of how we're shaping a world that favors peace and prosperity. With our European allies, we revitalized NATO and increased our cooperation on everything from counterterrorism to missile defense."

Of course our illustrious friend did not say a word about the urgent need to prevent global warming from rapidly increasing, or the catastrophic rains and snow that have just struck the world, or the food crisis that now threatens 80 countries of the Third World, and of course the tens of millions of tons of corn and soybeans that large US companies are devoting to the production of biofuel, while the world's population, already at 6.9 billion, will rise to 7 billion within 18 months.

The US president then stated that in March he would travel to Brazil, Chile and El Salvador "to forge new alliances across the Americas."

In Brazil, of course, he will be able to learn of the devastation and the deaths and disappearances caused by the unprecedented rains that have just taken place in Rio de Janeiro and Sao Paulo. It will undoubtedly be an opportunity for self-criticism of the fact that the United States refused to sign the Kyoto agreement, and that Obama's own government has promoted the suicidal policy of Copenhagen.

In Chile, the politics now get complicated. Presumably, tribute should be paid to Salvador Allende and to the thousands of Chileans murdered under the dictatorship of Pinochet, imposed on Chile by the United States. This is compounded by what I should also explain next. Another embarrassing situation is expected to occur in El Salvador, where the United States supplied weapons and forces trained and educated in US counterinsurgency military schools, tortured and committed horrible crimes against the combatants of the FMLN, whose party won the electoral vote most recently [in 2009].

Therefore, it is almost impossible to believe what the president says: "Around the globe, we're standing with those who take responsibility—helping farmers grow more food, supporting doctors who care for the sick…"

Many people know what the United States did with our doctors in Venezuela and other Latin American countries, hatching plans to promote defections and offering visas and money in the United States to abandon their difficult and dedicated work. Everybody knows about the free-trade agreements and the massive subsidies on US agricultural products designed to ruin the cereal and grain producers in Latin America. With these practices they ruined the production of cereals and maize in Mexico, making it dependent on US agriculture.

In countries as poor as Haiti, which supplied nearly all its own rice, the transnational companies ruined the local production with its subsidized surpluses and kept the country from producing this commodity and providing employment to thousands of Haitian workers.

Now it turns out, according to Obama's speech, the United States is the Olympic champion of medical aid and administrative honesty in the world. These issues are extensive and difficult to include in a single reflection.

We recall that the industrialized countries are the main looters of physicians and research scientists of the Third World. The US military budget exceeds that of all the other countries combined, its arms exports are double or triple if compared to those of the other states; their deployed nuclear arsenals number over 5,000 strategic weapons; it has more than 500 military bases overseas; its nuclear aircraft carriers and naval fleet dominate the seas of the planet. Is the American dream to be a model for the world? Who is the president of the United States trying to fool with that speech?

In the final part of his delirious message he concluded: "Thank you. God bless you, and may God bless the United States of America."

It is difficult for God to bless so many lies.

January 27, 2011

The Nato Plan to Occupy Libya

Oil has become the principal wealth in the hands of the great Yankee transnationals; through this energy source they have had an instrument that has considerably expanded their political power in the world. It was their main weapon when they readily decided to liquidate the Cuban revolution as soon as the first just and sovereign laws were passed in our homeland by depriving it of oil.

Today's civilization was developed on this energy source. Venezuela was the nation in this hemisphere that paid the highest price. The United States became the lord and master of the huge oil fields that Mother Nature had bestowed upon that sister country.

At the end of the last World War, it started to extract greater amounts of oil from the oil fields of Iran, as well as those in Saudi Arabia, Iraq and the surrounding Arab countries. These became their main suppliers. World consumption progressively increased to the unbelievable figure of approximately 80 million barrels a day, including what is extracted from United States territory, to which later gas, hydro and nuclear energies were added. Until the beginning of the 20th century, coal had been the basic source of energy that made possible industrial development, before billions of automobiles and engines consuming the liquid fuel were produced.

The squandering of oil and gas is associated with one of the greatest tragedies, which is far from being resolved, which is suffered by humankind: climate change.

When our revolution arose, Algeria, Libya and Egypt were not yet oil producers and a great part of the abundant reserves of Saudi Arabia, Iraq, Iran and the United Arab Emirates were still to be discovered.

In December 1951, Libya became the first African country to attain its independence after WW II, during which its territory was the stage for important battles between the troops of Germany and the United Kingdom, conferring fame and glory on Generals Erwin Rommel and Bernard L. Montgomery.

Ninety-five percent of its territory is completely made up of desert. Technology permitted the discovery of vital oilfields of excellent quality light oil that today produce 1.8 million barrels a day along with abundant deposits of natural gas. Such riches allowed Libya to achieve a life expectancy that is almost 75 years of age and the highest per capita income in Africa. Its harsh desert is located over an enormous lake of water reserves, equivalent to more than three times the land area of Cuba; this has made it possible to construct a broad network of pipelines of fresh water that stretch from one end of the country to the other.

Libya, which had one million inhabitants when it attained independence, today has somewhat more than 6 million.

The Libyan revolution took place in September 1969. Its main leader was Muammar al-Gaddafi, a soldier of Bedouin origin who, in his early years, was inspired by the ideas of the Egyptian leader Gamal Abdel Nasser. Without any doubt, many of his decisions are related to the changes that occurred when, as in Egypt, a weak and corrupt monarchy was overthrown in Libya.

The inhabitants of that country have an age-old warrior tradition. It is said that ancient Libyans were a part of Hannibal's army when he was at the point of destroying Ancient Rome with the troops that crossed the Alps.

One can agree or disagree with Gaddafi. The world has been bombarded with all kinds of news reports, especially in the mass media. It is necessary to wait for a period of time in order to learn precisely what is the truth and what are lies, or a mixture of all kinds of events that, in the midst of chaos, occurred in Libya. For me, what is absolutely clear is that the US government is not in the least concerned about creating peace in Libya and it will not hesitate in giving NATO the order to invade that rich country, perhaps in a matter of hours or a few short days.

Those who with pernicious intentions invented the lie that Gaddafi was headed for Venezuela, just as they did yesterday afternoon (Sunday February 20), today received a fitting response from Venezuela's Foreign Affairs Minister Nicolás Maduro who explicitly stated that he was "hoping that the Libyan people would find, in the exercise of their sovereignty, a peaceful solution to their difficulties, that would preserve the integrity of the Libyan people and nation, without the interference of imperialism..."

As for me, I cannot imagine that the Libyan leader would abandon his country, escaping responsibility [for what has happened], whether or not the charges [against him] are partially or totally false.

An honest person will always be against any injustice being committed against any people in the world. And, at this moment, the worst thing would be to remain silent in the face of the crime that NATO is getting ready to commit against the Libyan people.

The leadership of that war-mongering organization will attack Libya. We must condemn it!

February 21, 2011

The "Partnership of Equals" in Latin America

Saturday evening [February 19, 2011], after a sumptuous banquet, NATO leaders ordered the attack on Libya.

Of course, nothing could occur without the United States playing its unchallenged role as supreme leader. From NATO's command post in Europe, a senior official declared that "Odyssey Dawn" was about to begin.

World public opinion was deeply touched by the tragedy in Japan. The number of victims of the earthquake, the tsunami and the nuclear accident has continued to grow. At this point in time, there are thousands of dead, missing and affected by radiation. Resistance to the use of nuclear energy will also grow significantly.

The world is suffering, at the same time, the consequences of climate change; shortages and rising food prices, military spending and the squandering of natural and human resources are increasing. War [in Libya] was the most timely event that could occur at this time.

Obama's trip through Latin America receded into the background, and received hardly any attention. In Brazil, the contradictory interests between the United States and this sister nation have become evident. We cannot forget that Rio de Janeiro competed with Chicago to host the 2016 Olympic Games.

Obama wanted to win over the South American giant. He spoke of the "extraordinary rise of Brazil" that has made its mark on the international scene and he praised its economy as one of the economies with the fastest growth rate in the world; but he showed not even the least commitment to supporting Brazil as a permanent member of the privileged UN Security Council.

The Brazilian president [Dilma Rouseff] did not hesitate to express her disagreement with the protectionist measures the United States is applying against Brazil with the tariffs and subsidies that have constituted a mighty obstacle for the economy of that country.

Argentine writer Atilio Boron states that "what interests [Obama] most as administrator of the empire is advancing control of the Amazon region. The main requisite of this plan is to slow down, since it is something he cannot stop, the growing political and economic coordination and integration that is happening in the region; this had been very important in sinking ALCA in 2005 and frustrating the secessionist conspiracy and coups in Bolivia in 2008 and Ecuador in 2010. He also has to try to sow the seeds of discord between the most radical governments in the region (Cuba, Venezuela, Bolivia and Ecuador) and the "progressive" governments, mainly Brazil, Argentina and Uruguay…

"For the boldest US strategists, the Amazon river basin, like the Antarctic, is a free-access area where national sovereignties are not recognized…"

Tomorrow Obama moves on to Chile. His arrival is preceded by an interview he gave to the newspaper *El Mercurio* that was printed today [Sunday March 20] in which he confesses that the "Debate in the Americas," as he calls it, is based on a "partnership of equals" with Latin America. This practically leaves us breathless as we recall the Alliance for Progress that preceded the mercenary Bay of Pigs expedition [in 1961].

Obama explicitly states that the US vision for the hemisphere is based on the concept of a "partnership of equals" that he has pursued ever since becoming president of the United States. He stated that he will also focus on specific areas where they can work together, such as economic growth, energy, security and human rights.

This vision, he emphasized, has the aim of "improving common security, expanding economic opportunities, ensuring a clean energy future and supporting the democratic values we share... [and] promoting a safe, stable and prosperous Hemisphere where the United States and their partners share responsibilities on key regional and global issues..."

As we can see, everything is just so beautiful, worthy of being buried, along with Reagan's secrets, to be published in 200 years' time.

[...]

We have to ask Obama only one question. Remembering that one of his illustrious predecessors, Richard Nixon promoted the [September 11, 1973] coup that led to the heroic death of Salvador Allende, the torture and murder of thousands of persons, would Mr. Obama ask the forgiveness of the Chilean people?

March 20, 2011

The Assassination of Osama Bin Laden

Those who are familiar with these issues know that on September 11, 2001, our people expressed its solidarity with the US people and offered our modest cooperation in the area of health whereby we could have aided the victims of the brutal attack against the Twin Towers in New York.

We also immediately opened our country's airports to the US planes that were unable to land anywhere, given the chaos that developed immediately after the attack.

The Cuban revolution's traditional stand, which was always to oppose any action that jeopardized the lives of civilians, is well known.

Although we resolutely supported the armed struggle against Batista's dictatorship, we were, as a matter of principle, opposed to any terrorist action that could cause the death of innocent people. This position, which has been maintained for more than half a century, gives us the right to express our views about such a sensitive matter.

On that day, at a public gathering that took place at Ciudad Deportiva, I expressed my conviction that international terrorism could never be eradicated through violence and war.

By the way, Bin Laden was, for many years, a friend of the United States, a country that gave him military training; he was also an adversary of the Soviet Union and socialism. Whatever the actions attributed to him, the assassination of an unarmed human being while surrounded by his own relatives is something abhorrent. Apparently this is what the government of the most powerful nation that has ever existed did in Pakistan.

In the carefully drafted speech announcing Bin Laden's death Obama asserted the following:

> "And yet we know that the worst images are those that were unseen by the world. The empty seat at the dinner table. Children who were forced to grow up without their mother or their father. Parents who would never know the feeling of their child's embrace. Nearly 3,000 citizens taken from us, leaving a gaping hole in our hearts."

This paragraph expressed a dramatic truth, but cannot prevent honest people from remembering the unjust wars unleashed by the United States in Iraq and Afghanistan, the hundreds of thousands of children forced to grow up without their mothers and fathers and the parents who would never know the feeling of their child's embrace.

Millions of citizens were removed from their villages in Iraq, Afghanistan, Vietnam, Laos, Cambodia, Cuba and many other countries of the world.

Still engraved on the minds of hundreds of millions of people are also the horrible images of human beings who, for months and even for years, have been submitted to unbearable and excruciating torture in Guantánamo, an illegally occupied territory in Cuba. They were kidnapped and transferred to secret prisons with the hypocritical connivance of supposedly civilized societies.

Obama has no way to conceal the fact that Osama was executed in front of his children and wives, who are now in the custody of the authorities of Pakistan, a Muslim country of almost 200 million inhabitants, whose laws have been violated, its national dignity offended and its religious traditions desecrated.

How can he now prevent the women and children of the person who was executed outside of any law and without any trial from explaining what happened? How could he prevent those images from being broadcast to the world?

[…]

Now, by assassinating Bin Laden and plunging his corpse into the deep sea, they have demonstrated their fear and insecurity and turned him into a far more dangerous person.

After the initial euphoria, US public opinion will end up becoming critical of the methods that, far from protecting its citizens, will enhance feelings of hatred and revenge against them.

May 4, 2011

CUBAN REVOLUTION READER

A Documentary History of Fidel Castro's Revolution

Edited by Julio García Luis

The Cuban revolution was one of the defining moments of the 20th century, its influence reaching far beyond the shores of the tiny Caribbean island.

This book documents the turbulent 50-year history of Fidel Castro's revolution, from the euphoria of the early years to near economic collapse in the 1990s, and finally the Cuban leader's decision to step down in 2008.

In his introduction, Julio García Luis, offers a critical examination of Cuba's decades-long relationship with the Soviet Union and the epilogue considers the prospects for the revolution without Fidel Castro.

Including a comprehensive chronology and index, this is an essential resource for scholars and others.

ISBN 978-1-920888-89-3 (paper)

GUANTÁNAMO

Why the Illegal US Base Should be Returned to Cuba

Fidel Castro

How is it that territory around Guantánamo Bay, seized after the Spanish-American War over 100 years ago, is still held by the United States as a naval base? President Obama has proposed to close the prison for those captured in the "war against terrorism," but Fidel Castro argues here that the illegal occupation of the territory must end immediately.

With a foreword by Noam Chomsky, this book also features a comprehensive chronology of the base's history and extensive appendices, including some key historical documents through which Washington has justified its continued occupation and recently declassified documents from the 1962 Missile Crisis.

"Imagine if after we defeated the British in our revolution, we then let them keep a few thousand troops and a bunch of battleships in New York Harbor. Weird!"
—Michael Moore

ISBN 978-0-9804292-5-1 (paper)

FURTHER READING FROM OCEAN PRESS

FIDEL CASTRO READER

Edited by David Deutschmann and Deborah Shnookal

An outstanding new anthology of one of history's greatest orators

At last! A comprehensive selection of one of the 20th century's most influential political figures and one of history's greatest orators, Fidel Castro.

Opening with Fidel's famous courtroom defense speech following the 1953 attack on the Moncada garrison, this anthology includes more than five decades of Fidel's outstanding oratory, right up to his recent reflections on the future of the Cuban revolution "post-Fidel."

With an extensive chronology on the Cuban revolution, a comprehensive index and 24 pages of photos, this is an essential resource for scholars, researchers and general readers.

As new leaders and social forces emerge in Latin America today, this book sheds light on the continent's future as well as its past.

"Fidel's devotion to the word is almost magical." —Gabriel García Márquez

"Fidel is the leader of one of the smallest countries in the world, but he has helped to shape the destinies of millions of people across the globe." —Angela Davis

"Fidel Castro is a man of the masses... The Cuban revolution has been a source of inspiration to all freedom-loving people." —Nelson Mandela

ISBN 978-1-920888-88-6 (paper)

Also available in Spanish ISBN 978-1-921438-01-1

oceanpress

e-mail info@oceanbooks.com.au

www.oceanbooks.com.au